What Is Man?

What Is Man?

A Biblical Understanding of Humanity and Why It Matters Today

LENARD TAVERNELLI

Foreword by Thomas R. Schreiner

WIPF & STOCK • Eugene, Oregon

WHAT IS MAN?
A Biblical Understanding of Humanity and Why It Matters Today

Wipf & Stock
An Imprint of Wipf and Stock Publishers
199 W. 8th Ave., Suite 3
Eugene, OR 97401

www.wipfandstock.com

PAPERBACK ISBN: 979-8-3852-6965-5
HARDCOVER ISBN: 979-8-3852-6966-2
EBOOK ISBN: 979-8-3852-6967-9

VERSION NUMBER 02/06/26

To Angela
My faithful wife and true helper (Gen 2:18)

And to Bethel Community Church, Chicago
"One new man" in Christ (Eph 2:15)

Contents

Foreword

CONFUSION ABOUNDS TODAY ON what it means to be a human being, or more specifically what it means to be a man or woman or a boy or girl. Many people in our culture would be astonished to discover the fundamental reason for our confusion, but John Calvin at the outset of *The Institutes of the Christian Religion* identified the root issue long ago. Calvin remarks,

> Our wisdom, in so far as it ought to be deemed true and solid Wisdom, consists almost entirely of two parts: the knowledge of God and of ourselves. But as these are connected together by many ties, it is not easy to determine which of the two precedes and gives birth to the other. For, in the first place, no man can survey himself without forthwith turning his thoughts towards the God in whom he lives and moves; because it is perfectly obvious, that the endowments which we possess cannot possibly be from ourselves; nay, that our very being is nothing else than subsistence in God alone.[1]

Calvin considers knowledge of ourselves, and he rightly says that knowledge of ourselves is inextricably intertwined with knowing God. Indeed, the connection between knowing God and ourselves is thick and complicated, such that we can't easily determine which comes first. I am not concerned with the questions of order and precedence here. My purpose is simpler. Calvin reminds us that we won't know ourselves, we won't understand what it means to be a human being, if we don't know God. We can trace the modern

1. Calvin, *Institutes* 1.1.1.

misunderstandings of what it means to be human to a failure to know God. When we don't acknowledge the Creator, we can't grasp the identity and purpose of the creature.

Lenard Tavernelli's book is a welcome response to the ignorance about human beings that reigns, sometimes even in our churches. He takes us on a wonderful tour of the scriptural teaching about what it means to be human, and he rightly begins with God, with the truth that God created us. From there he turns to Jesus Christ, who is the model human being, the only human being who lived life every moment as God intended it be lived. As Tavernelli reminds us, he is our Savior and Lord, the one who rescues us through his atoning death and victorious resurrection from the sin that deforms and defaces us. But Jesus is also our example, showing us what it means to live a fully human life, and we do so when we trust in and obey the Lord.

One of the remarkable features of this book is its compactness. It doesn't take long to read, but at the same time it is packed with biblical truth, and yet it is written in a way that is inviting and accessible. We learn along the way about the nature of human beings: that we are creatures with a body and soul. In addition, the crucial issue of what it means to be male or female is explicated and unpacked. Sin and redemption, vocation and culture, marriage and singleness are all investigated. At the same time, Tavernelli concludes with our ultimate purpose, reminding us that we were made to glorify God and enjoy him forever. We cannot be and will not be fulfilled in our humanity unless we are rightly related to God.

Thomas R. Schreiner
James Buchanan Harrison Professor of New Testament Interpretation
The Southern Baptist Theological Seminary

Preface

THEY SAY THAT "NECESSITY is the mother of invention." I'm not trying to "invent" the doctrine of man, and I don't have to. I am, however, attempting to write a simple, accessible book on the biblical doctrine of man that isn't intimidating for everyday Christians to read. I'm a pastor, and I want the people I shepherd to be able to think biblically about what it means to be human. If anthropology (the study of humankind) is the biggest challenge facing the church in the twenty-first century and the third millennium of the Christian age, then many of the questions we face are directly related to our understanding of what it means to be human. Many of the problems and challenges we face in the world today come from misunderstandings of what it means to be human. Therefore, Christians, all Christians, not just pastors and scholars, must understand what it means to be human and how to answer the questions they will inevitably face and that people will ask them in their families, workplaces, schools, and communities.

As Anthony Hoekema says, "It is difficult to exaggerate the importance of the doctrine of man."[2] If that was true when Hoekema wrote over three decades ago, how much more do we need to be clear about what it means to be human with the challenges we face today due to the changes in worldview throughout our society and the new technologies outpacing ethics. That's why I see the need for a book such as this one. Yet as I've looked for one, I couldn't find one. Yes, there are very good books available on the subject of what the Bible says about what it means to be human,

2. Hoekema, *Created in God's Image*, 1.

but they're either too long or inaccessible for most people, who aren't going to Bible college or seminary. In fact, simple books on the doctrine of man are either hard to find or out of print. As I prepared to teach the church I pastor on this doctrine, and with the current cultural moment, I find this lack of such resources unacceptable. So, I have written this book that I hope is clear, simple, and, above all, biblical. I pray that the Lord will bless my efforts for the good of his people and the glory of his name.

Acknowledgments

Thank you to Jared Von Kamp, Paul Springer, Saolomon Mouacheupao, and Elida Gonzalez for helping to proofread this book. You have been faithful friends.

Thank you to Dr. Thomas Schreiner, my former pastor and seminary professor, for reading this book and writing the foreword.

Thank you to the saints of Bethel Community Church, Chicago, who have allowed me to serve as pastor and teach on the biblical view of humanity that started this project.

I would especially like to thank my wife, Angela, for proofreading, providing helpful advice, and allowing me to complete this book. You are truly a gift from God.

Introduction

A Question Worth Asking (and Answering)

WHAT IS MAN? A complex, organic machine? Chemical interactions and reactions? A highly evolved animal? Stardust? Something, or someone, else? How can we tell the difference between a highly developed AI (artificial intelligence) humanoid and a human person? How we answer the basic questions about what it means to be human will determine how we answer many of the questions and challenges facing us today.

In Psalm 8:4, Israel's great king, David, asks, "What is man that you [God] are mindful of him?" David isn't some secular pagan philosopher pondering the deep questions of life and trying to come up with his own answers. Rather, David knows the answer because he has God's word. Specifically, he had the book of Genesis that provides the answer to that question. David isn't speculating but meditating. And through his meditation, David is drawn to worship God as he considers God's awesome creation and the amazing design and purpose God has given mankind.

David's response is profound:

> You [God] have made him a little lower than the heavenly beings and crowned him with glory and honor. You have given him dominion over the works of your hands; you have put all things under his feet, all sheep and oxen, and also the beasts of the field, the birds of the heavens, and the fish of the sea, whatever passes along the paths of the seas. (Ps 8:5–8)

David draws from Genesis 1–2, celebrating God's wisdom, then concludes by worshiping God: "O LORD, our Lord, how majestic is your name in all the earth" (Ps 8:9).

Like David, I'm going to start with God and the Bible as my final authority to answer the question "What is man?" I will provide a question that each chapter answers, and then I will attempt to provide an accessible answer to what a biblical understanding of man is, why a biblical understanding of man is important to the challenges we face today, and how this biblical understanding of man answers those challenges. As I do so, I hope to draw from important Christian works and point you, the reader, to them if you want a more in-depth, scholarly answer. I will also show how a biblical understanding of man applies to how we live today. Ultimately, my goal is that you will walk away humbly worshiping the sovereign God who so wisely designed us for his purposes.

So where shall we begin? "In the beginning," right? Yes and no. King David drew from Genesis 1–2 in his meditations that led to penning Psalm 8. David knew mankind, male and female, was created in (or according to) the image and likeness of God to have dominion over the cosmos and everything in it (Gen 1:26–28). However, as Christians, we have Jesus Christ: the Word made flesh (John 1:14). We have a fuller revelation than David did because we have all sixty-six books of the Bible. More than that, God has revealed himself fully and finally in Jesus Christ (Heb 1:1–2). As Colossians 1:15 says, "He [Jesus Christ] is the image of the invisible God, the firstborn of all creation." And God is conforming his people to the likeness of Jesus Christ so that he may be "the firstborn among many brothers" (Rom 8:29).

Since Jesus is the God-Man, he is *the Man*—all that God created man to be. He is the pattern and the ultimate Man after whom God has created humans and is new-creating his redeemed people. So we will begin with Jesus, the One by whom, through whom, and for whom everything exists (Col 1:16). And while I will try to lay everything out in an orderly (systematic) fashion, when possible, I will also try to quickly explain texts and show how they lead to the conclusions I propose. As I do so, I hope that you, the reader, will have a better understanding of what it means to be a human person and how to live God's way in God's world as the pinnacle of his creation.

I pray the result of this brief work will be that you will love people, created in God's image, more—but not just humans as a concept. My goal is that you will love individual people, your neighbor, as yourself (Matt 22:39). My goal is that you will see every human being and love every human being, no matter who he/she is and no matter what he/she does because of who and what he/she is. Most of all, I pray that you will love supremely the God who created us, and like David, you will worship him and honor him: both gathered with his church and in all that you do in all of life.

1

Created by God

While the popular "scientific" (read: naturalistic) myth of our day is that humans are highly evolved animals, this is not the only story of human origins. Every culture throughout history has had a story regarding human origins that explains what humans are and where we came from. When I was in college, I learned about ancient Near Eastern creation myths, like the Enuma Elish, a Babylonian myth. My professors claimed that this creation account is so similar to the account in Genesis 1–2 that the Bible must have borrowed from it and other such myths. In the Enuma Elish, Marduk defeats Tiamat in battle and then makes humans out of the blood of Quingu, another god.[1] If you've ever read Genesis and Enuma Elish side by side, like me, you probably weren't struck by all the similarities but all the differences between the two.

With the many different answers to our origins, you may wonder, "Who are you to tell someone what it means to be human?

1. Mark, "Enuma Elish." We should not be surprised by some similarities between creation stories from the ancient Near East and the biblical account in Genesis. For one reason, Moses was probably aware of these myths and may have written to intentionally counter their teachings with the truth. Another reason the accounts will have similarities is because they are written in similar times within a similar culture. And a third reason for similarities is because humans have a collective memory, passing on remembered (though often distorted) facts (such as the various flood accounts).

Who has the authority, the right to answer that question?" To understand what it means to be human, we must begin by answering this question about authority.

In contrast to evolutionary theory and other truth claims, the Bible is clear that "in the beginning, God created the heavens and the earth" (Gen 1:1; see also Rev 4:11) *ex nihilo* (Latin for "out of nothing"). Then, through his powerful spoken word, God formed the earth and filled it in six days (Gen 1:3–25). In the New Testament, we learn that the Architect and Agent of creation is the eternal Word. "In the beginning was the Word, and the Word was with God, and the Word was God. He was in the beginning with God. All things were made through him, and without him was not any thing made that was made" (John 1:1–3). This person who created the world and made it an orderly, structured cosmos is none other than God the Son who took on flesh, becoming fully man, the Man Christ Jesus (John 1:14, Col 1:15–17).

In the accounts of Jesus' birth in the Gospels according to Matthew and Luke, the writers describe how God didn't create Jesus by natural processes of procreation. Instead, God supernaturally intervened by his Spirit (the same Spirit who hovered over the great deep in Gen 1:2) to form the human in the womb of Mary, the body and soul of the person of his Son, Jesus Christ (Matt 1:18, Luke 1:35). God is not an aloof landlord or watchmaker. He doesn't just set things in motion and sit back. He can and does act in his creation as he pleases when he pleases, whether in the beginning or "in the fullness of time" (Gal 4:4) to supernaturally create or to begin a "new creation" in and through his Son, Jesus (see 2 Cor 5:17, Rev 3:14).

Returning to Genesis, we're told that God made mankind, male and female, in his image and likeness (Gen 1:26–27). While I will consider what that phrase means in chapter 3, I must begin by establishing the biblical truth: God created mankind. Yes, God formed and fashioned the first man, Adam, out of the dust of the ground. Adam did not somehow evolve from lower animals through a process of macroevolution. From a natural reading of the text, the Bible doesn't allow such an explanation. Rather, God supernaturally created Adam (and Eve) by intervening in his creation.[2] And he created the first humans to dwell in his presence and have dominion over the cosmos.

God describes this process of supernatural intervention in creation in Genesis 2, where God describes what became of the heavens and earth that he created in Genesis 1:1—2:3. In Genesis 2:7, after creating the earth and preparing it to be a home for people, "then the Lord God formed the man of dust from the ground and breathed into his nostrils the breath of life, and the man became a living creature." God made the man, but it wasn't until God breathed "the breath of life" into Adam that he became a living being. The Hebrew word for "living creature" is *nephesh*, and it is used for other living creatures (animals) as well (Gen 2:19). God supernaturally made the first man, but he didn't stop there.

God created a suitable helper for the man. You've probably heard, "Men are from Mars, women are from Venus." The idea is men and women are so different from one another that we originated from different planets and met in the middle (Earth). Now, men and women are very different in a lot of ways, but what should strike us from the biblical account is how similar men and women are. While Adam was created from the dust of the ground, like other animals (Gen 2:19), God is clear that humans and animals are very different—so different that animals don't make a "helper fit for" man (Gen 2:18; sorry, pet lovers). Therefore, God supernaturally acted again. This time he didn't create a new human out of the dust of the ground but a woman out of the side of the man (Gen 2:21–22). And since the man and woman are so similar, Adam composed the first human song (or poem)—a love song/poem about his new partner, woman. "This at last is bone of my bones and flesh of my flesh; she shall be called Woman [Hebrew: *isha*], because she was taken out of Man [Hebrew: *ish*]" (Gen 2:23).

2. This is not a matter of science versus nonscience but a naturalistic worldview versus a supernatural worldview. For further study, see Creation Ministries International (https://creation.com/) or Answers in Genesis (https://answersingenesis.org/).

Why does it matter that man is created by God? One of the biggest issues in our day is the matter of authority. Ultimately, God has authority over everything about every human and every nation. God "made from one man every nation of mankind to live on all the face of the earth, having determined allotted periods and the boundaries of their dwelling place" (Acts 17:26). Recognizing God created humanity means that God alone can define who we are as a race and as individual human persons. This implies that God's special revelation, the Bible, is the final authority—self or social groups do not have the final say.

While the rejection of authority may take on many forms, one of the hallmarks of our current culture has been called *expressive individualism*: "Each of us finds our meaning by giving expression to our own feelings and desires."[3] Since our modern (postmodern) culture claims individuals have the right (authority) to define self, everyone else in society and the world must not only tolerate but recognize and celebrate one's individualist expressions (whatever they may be) or face the charge of causing "harm."[4] Since the individual and society recognizes no absolute authority (and therefore, no absolute standards) beyond the individual or social group, this is the logical (or illogical) outcome.

We Christians can only give a sufficient answer to the confusion and chaos in our culture today by acknowledging that humans are created by God and that he alone has the right to define who we are. In a society that exhorts, "Just follow your heart," and that encourages (demands) everyone to do as he/she feels, we can only have solid ground to stand on against the strong cultural currents by recognizing that we're created beings under God's authority.

While Adam and Eve rejected God's authority and opened "Pandora's box," so to speak, Jesus, the new and better Adam, consciously lived under the authority of his Father in heaven (see John 5:19, 30; 8:28–29). He both obeyed the Father for us—that is, on our behalf as our representative—and he obeyed the Father as the

3. This term comes from Charles Taylor. The quote is from Carl Trueman (Trueman, *Rise and Triumph*, 46).

4. Trueman, *Rise and Triumph*, 54.

pattern for us (as our example). In this way, Jesus lived the most truly human life because only Jesus lived completely under God's authority.

Recognizing God created us and exercises his rightful, good, loving authority over us should lead to a response of humble obedience and worship. Consider the wisdom and knowledge and power required to make the creation, especially humans. In pondering the intricacies of God's creation of man, David responds, "Such knowledge is too wonderful for me; it is high; I cannot attain it" (Ps 139:6). He continues, "I praise you, for I am fearfully and wonderfully made. Wonderful are your works; my soul knows it very well" (Ps 139:14). We ought to stand in awe of God and praise him for his marvelous work of creating us as persons in his image and likeness.

2

Jesus Christ: The Model Man

If someone asks you, "What is God's purpose for creating the world (including humans)?" how would you answer? What does the Bible say is God's ultimate purpose for creation? Colossians 1:16 tells us, "All things were created through [Jesus Christ] and for him." God's purpose in the universe is "to unite all things in [Jesus Christ], things in heaven and things on earth" (Eph 1:10). And God saves for himself a people to conform them "to the image of his Son, in order that he might be the firstborn among many brothers" (Rom 8:29). Do you see a pattern? God's purpose is to exalt and glorify his Son, Jesus Christ. God's purpose is for Jesus Christ to be Lord of all and for redeemed persons to display the likeness of Jesus Christ because he is *the image of God* (Col 1:15).

Jesus Christ is the pattern for all humanity. He is the measure and the standard. So how can we understand Jesus? In AD 451, the Council of Chalcedon adopted the Chalcedonian Creed. It is the orthodox definition of who Jesus Christ is.[1] As Michael Wilkinson

1. The Chalcedonian Creed says, "We then, following the holy Fathers, all with one consent, teach men to confess one and the same Son, our Lord Jesus Christ, the same perfect in Godhead and also perfect in manhood; truly God and truly man, of a reasonable soul and body; consubstantial [of one substance] with the Father according to the Godhead, and consubstantial with us according to the Manhood; in all things like unto us, without sin; begotten before all ages of the Father according to the Godhead, and in these latter days, for us and for our

argues, the definition of Jesus Christ as the God-Man in the creed helps us to understand what it means to be human, since Jesus is the pattern for what it means to be human.[2]

The creed says Jesus is "perfect [complete] in manhood; . . . truly man, of a reasonable soul and body." Jesus is not mostly man or like man but fully and completely man. He is truly man, one of us. Jesus is both body and soul in nature. He is of one substance ("consubstantial") with the Father and "at the same time consubstantial [of one substance] with us" regarding his humanity. As the creed explains, Jesus is "in all things like unto us, without sin." This is why we see in Jesus true and perfect manhood: he's human in every way as we are. Yet, Jesus is humanity without sin (Heb 4:15). That's because God did not create humans with sin. Sin is not essential to humanity. The redeemed will continue to be humans forever in the new heaven and new earth, yet without sin.

As the creed continues, Jesus exists "in two natures, [without confusion], unchangeably, indivisibly, inseparably." He has a complete and truly divine nature as well as a complete and truly human nature. Yet, he is not "two persons." He is "one and the same Son, and only begotten, God the Word, the Lord Jesus Christ." Jesus is one person. He is God the Son with a fully human nature.

As we'll consider more fully in chapter 4, it's important to recognize the distinction between person and nature. We see in Jesus one person (God the Son). The person of Jesus is eternal. His divine nature is eternal. But this one person, God the Son, took on

---

salvation, born of the Virgin Mary, the Mother of God, according to the Manhood; one and the same Christ, Son, Lord, Only-begotten, to be acknowledged in two natures, inconfusedly [without confusion], unchangeably, indivisibly, inseparably; the distinction of natures being by no means taken away by the union, but rather the property of each nature being persevered, and concurring in one Person and one Subsistence, not parted or divided into two persons, but one and the same Son, and only begotten, God the Word, the Lord Jesus Christ, as the prophets from the beginning have declared concerning him, as the Lord Jesus Christ himself has taught us, and the Creed of the holy Fathers has handed down to us" (Grudem, *Systematic Theology*, 1169–70).

2. See Wilkinson, *Crowned with Glory and Honor*, 39–121, for an in-depth explanation of why we should define what it means to be human in Jesus Christ. Also see Wilkinson, "What Is Man?"

a second nature, a human nature, when he became Man and was conceived of Mary when she was a virgin. As Philippians 2:6–7 explains, "Though he was in the form of God, [Christ Jesus] did not count equality with God a thing to be grasped, but emptied himself, by taking the form of a servant, being born in the likeness of men." Jesus emptied himself not by subtracting from his infinite divine nature but by adding to himself a finite human nature.

Only by becoming completely and truly human can he completely and truly save us. If Jesus lacked a human body or soul, as ancient heresies taught, Jesus could not save those aspects of our nature that he lacked. The substitutionary sacrifice to save us from our sins could be made only by one who is truly and completely human. A sinless man had to die for the forgiveness of sins of humans. As Michael Wilkinson writes, "The divine Son became the man Jesus Christ so that his substitutionary sacrifice would actually remove the sins of his new covenant people. Thus, being a truly and fully human being is an ontological requirement for Christ to succeed as the Redeemer of man."[3] Through the saving acts of the person of the Son of God as man, Jesus fully and truly saves the whole human person from the penalty and power of sin.

Considering the infinite wisdom and knowledge of God displayed in the gospel should cause us to respond in heartfelt worship, as we see the apostle Paul do. "Oh, the depth of the riches and wisdom and knowledge of God! How unsearchable are his judgments and how inscrutable his ways! For who has known the mind of the Lord, or who has been his counselor? Or who has given a gift to him that he might be repaid? For from him and through him and to him are all things. To him be glory forever. Amen" (Rom 11:33–36).

Since Jesus Christ is the pattern for our humanity, we should look to Jesus as he's revealed to us in Scripture to understand what it means to be completely and truly human. If we look to something or someone other than Jesus as he's presented in the Bible, our understanding of what it means to be human will be less than truly and fully biblical. Understanding the full biblical picture of

3. Wilkinson, *Crowned with Glory and Honor*, 78.

humanity requires us to start with Jesus to define what it means to be created in the image of God. Perhaps that is one reason Genesis does not define what it means by the "image" and "likeness" of God. The concepts of the image and likeness of God become fully defined only as God progressively reveals himself in Scripture unto the climax of revelation in the God-Man, Jesus Christ.

Looking to Jesus keeps us from falling into the modern dehumanizing understandings of humanity. We do not fall into the victim mentality of therapeutic man. Yes, Jesus was a victim of wicked humans when they crucified him. But Jesus took full responsibility for himself and his actions, even when he was mistreated. He continued to entrust himself to his Father's plan and to obey his Father even when he was sinned against (see 1 Pet 2:18–25). Real victims deserve real justice. But if we define everyone as oppressed victims, there can be no true justice because no one is finally responsible for his/her own actions, since everyone is always acting from his/her victimhood. Jesus' life demonstrates that humans, even when we are victims, are not merely victims of our circumstances but responsible agents.

Looking to Jesus also keeps us from falling into the evolutionary understanding of man as nothing but a chance-evolved primate. If we are the product of chance or fate (which is not the same thing as God's sovereignty), then we have no hope of a better future. Instead, we fall into the dystopian trap of believing humans are chemical machines that will one day be overtaken by AI machines (or perhaps annihilate ourselves accidentally or malevolently through nuclear or chemical warfare). But because Jesus' humanity defines our humanity, we recognize that humans are specially created in the image and likeness of God, so we are unique and irreplaceable. We can have confident hope that "if we have been united with [Jesus Christ] in a death like his, we shall certainly be united with him in a resurrection like his" (Rom 6:5). We are creatures of great dignity with the potential for eternal glory. Every human from the moment of conception *is* in the image and according to the likeness of God. It is to consider what it means to be image bearers that we now turn.

3

Created in God's Image and Likeness

People today may ask you, "What's so special about humans?" As a Christian, you may answer, "We're created in God's image and likeness." But what does it mean to be created in God's image and likeness? You may know that this phrase occurs in Genesis 1:26–28:

> Then God said, "Let us make man in our image, after our likeness. And let them have dominion over the fish of the sea and over the birds of the heavens and over the livestock and over all the earth and over every creeping thing that creeps on the earth." So God created man in his own image, in the image of God he created him; male and female he created them. And God blessed them. And God said to them, "Be fruitful and multiply and fill the earth and subdue it, and have dominion over the fish of the sea and over the birds of the heavens and over every living thing that moves on the earth."

But what does that passage of scripture mean?

Traditionally, some have taught that God's image is an aspect of being human. They believed that God's image is an element of our being (ontology). People have thought *the image of God* in man may be reason, having a free will, or morality (the ability to understand right from wrong). Others have thought *the image of God* refers to humanity's ability to have relationships, especially a relationship with God.

Recent studies have understood *the image of God* to refer to God's calling for mankind to have dominion (Gen 1:28). In the ancient Near East, rulers would set up images in their likeness, such as a statue to represent the ruler. Those images proclaimed to anyone in the realm who reigned there.

Recently, John Kilner argues that God's image isn't an aspect or attribute of humanity, and he's correct. Kilner argues, "*Actual* likeness to God is not what being created in God's image involves." Rather, he says, "God's expressed intention" is that humans evidence their "special connection" with God by meaningfully reflecting God by becoming like Jesus Christ.[1] Every human is equally made in the image of God, so every human person bears full dignity as a human being.

THE MEANING OF IMAGE AND LIKENESS

With the various understandings of the phrase *image and likeness*, we must be careful as we consider what this phrase and these words mean, as misunderstandings can and have been used throughout history to justify injustices against people who were deemed to be less than image bearers.[2] So what does it mean to be created in the image and likeness of God?

First, notice that Genesis declares that this is God's plan: "Then God said, 'Let us make man in our image, after our likeness'" (Gen 1:26). As we saw in chapter 1, humans are created by God. He's the Creator; we are the created. Therefore, God alone has the authority to define humanity.

Second, notice God's design. God planned to make man in his image and according to his likeness: "So God created man

1. Kilner, *Dignity and Destiny*, 79; emphasis original.

2. Examples include justifying mistreatment of women, slavery, and genocide.

in his own image, in the image of God he created him; male and female he created them" (Gen 1:27). Men and women are both created equally as God's image bearers.

Men and women are created *in* or *according to* God's image and likeness. While these two prepositions are similar in meaning, their meaning is not identical. To say humans are created *in* the image of God emphasizes the way "in which humans are closely like God," while *according to* refers to the way "humans are similar [to God] but distinct."[3] God created humans in his image as his royal representatives. He made humans in his likeness because we are like him, but we are not God. Since being a human is to be in God's image and likeness, having dominion is not what it means to be in God's image. Rather, humans have dominion over the cosmos and everything in it because we are created in God's image and likeness as his earthly representatives (Gen 1:28). Dominion is the result of being God's image bearers, not the definition of being image bearers.

We must be clear that the Bible never says that the image of God has to do with an aspect or attribute of our being. The Bible never says that reason or morality is what makes humans image bearers. Rather, to be human *is to be* made in the image of God. This is important, for example, because every human being, regardless of skin color, ethnicity,[4] gender, class, socioeconomic status, age, and mental or physical capacities (or incapacities) is fully

3. Gentry and Wellum, *Kingdom Through Covenant*, 198–200. While commentator Ken Mathews argues "there is no special distinction to be made between the different Hebrew prepositions" *in* the image of God and *according to* God's likeness, as the two terms are interchangeable in Genesis 5:2 (Mathews, *Genesis 1:1—11:26*, 167), Gentry and Wellum argue persuasively that Genesis 5:1–3 helps our understanding as we read of Adam's son, Seth. "This is the book of the generations of Adam. When God created man, he made him in the *likeness* of God. Male and female he created them, and he blessed them and named them Man when they were created. When Adam had lived 130 years, he fathered a son in his own *likeness*, after his *image*, and named him Seth" (Gen 5:1–3). Genesis 5 switches the order of the two prepositions because as his son, Seth is similar to Adam but not identical to him.

4. Racism is sin. But I prefer not to refer to various "races" of humanity because we are one race. We all come from Adam.

human and fully an image bearer. From conception, a person is in God's image and has full dignity.

As the image of God, humans are the rulers, representing God to the world. Being made in God's likeness speaks to our "sonship." As beings created according to the likeness of God, humans reflect God or display who God is and what he's like (we're to resemble God in all we do). We can relate to God, and we are *like* God.[5] That is why sin is so heinous. Every time we sin, we fail to represent God truly and rightly. When we sin, we lie about what God is like, falling short of God's glory and failing to glorify God as God (Rom 3:23).

Now notice God's purpose: "And let them [mankind] have dominion over the fish of the sea and over the birds of the heavens and over the livestock and over all the earth and over every creeping thing that creeps on the earth" (Gen 1:28). God created us in his image and likeness so that we can fulfill his purpose to have dominion over his cosmos. We're stewards of what belongs to God, so we're to reign with goodness, justice, and kindness toward all God has made, just as he reigns over us. We will consider this cultural mandate in greater detail in chapter 10.

As Genesis continues, God chooses a man named Abram, whom God renames "Abraham." Abraham is to be a new Adam to whom God will give a land and progeny who will have dominion (see Gen 12:1–3). Though Adam was a disobedient son who failed to trust God and brought curse and death upon the earth (Gen 3), through trusting in God and obeying him, Abraham will become the father of the nations of the world, and all the various families of the world will be blessed through him (Gen 12:3). God chose Abraham "that he may command his children and his household after him to keep the way of the LORD by doing righteousness and justice, so that the LORD may bring to Abraham what he has promised him" (Gen 18:19). It is through Abraham's greater Son, Jesus, that God will truly establish his reign on earth through a renewed humanity who will be in the likeness of God in Christ, to reign on

5. Gentry and Wellum, *Kingdom Through Covenant*, 191–95.

the earth with goodness, justice, and kindness (see Rom 8:29–30, Eph 5:1–2, Rev 5:9–10).

SO WHAT?

Based on what we've seen, every human being has inherent dignity and value because every human being is created in God's image and likeness. In our utilitarian age that measures people by their roles, abilities, net worth, intelligence, ingenuity, or social status, we must recover the doctrine that every human being is created in God's image. It is not okay to hurt or kill humans in the womb (through abortion in any form), nor to disregard humans who cannot contribute to the welfare of society as much as others due to some handicap (as we define welfare), nor to discard those humans who no longer have the same utilitarian abilities they once had (the elderly, infirm, etc.).

Recognizing that every human is created in the image and likeness of God has implications for how we treat foreigners (who are in a nation legally or illegally) and refugees. While a government has both a right and mandate to protect its own borders and citizens, humans do not have the right to mistreat other human beings. Jesus himself became a refugee and an alien in Egypt when his parents had to take him and flee to escape the murderous intentions of King Herod (Matt 2:13–15). And while Jesus was a Jewish man sent primarily to serve the Jewish people during his sojourn on earth, Jesus regularly cared for people of other ethnicities and treated them with respect, even if they were despised by his own people (see Mark 7:24–30, Luke 17:11–19, John 4). Jesus' care and respect fulfilled God's command to Israel to care for and respect foreigners living among them. God had commanded Israel, "When a stranger sojourns with you in your land, you shall not do him wrong. You shall treat the stranger who sojourns with you as the native among you, and you shall love him as yourself, for you were strangers in the land of Egypt: I am the Lord your God" (Lev 19:33–34). Because every human is created in God's image, we should treat him/her with dignity, even if he/she is a "stranger" who has entered borders illegally.

Likewise, recognizing we're created in the image and likeness of God also implies we're not to worship other humans or put them above God (Exod 20:3, Matt 22:37–38). Though sin cannot destroy the structures of creation, sin does distort, corrupt, and enslave people so that we think, speak, feel, act, and will in ways contrary to God's created order. We default to worshiping creatures rather than worshiping God (Rom 1:18–23). The result is that we do not exercise dominion faithfully but hurt and destroy and approve of injustice and unrighteousness for self-serving purposes (Rom 1:24–32).

Since humans are created in God's image, we likewise are not to make God in our own image and likeness, since that is a distortion of God and reversing of the proper Creator-creature relationship. We are not to make any image or likeness of God because humans are the living image bearers of the living God, and any other image of God is dead (Exod 20:4–6). As Greg Beale writes, we will become like what we worship "for restoration or for ruin."[6] So we must be careful to only worship God as he has revealed himself to us in Scripture, or we will become like the dead things we design and worship (Ps 115:4–8).

Certainly every human being has rights, but more than that, we are responsible for other humans. We're to love them because they're created in God's image (Matt 22:39–40). We must open our mouths for those being treated unjustly who cannot speak for themselves (Prov 31:8). This is part of our role as image bearers. And true societal justice can only be grounded in the truth that mankind is created in the image of God (Gen 9:5–6). Dominion over God's creation includes loving other image bearers because we first love the God who created them.

6. Beale, *We Become What We Worship*, 11.

4

Person and Nature

In the next chapter, we'll consider the body-soul nature of every human being. But before we do so, we must consider the distinction between human nature and human person. That may sound like a strange distinction to make, but this is a distinction that is made about Jesus, as we saw in chapter 2. The Chalcedonian Creed recognized that Jesus is one person in two natures: a divine nature and a human nature.[1] Since Jesus Christ is the pattern for what it means to be man, humans are, like Jesus, person and nature beings.

Do not misunderstand. By saying that humans are a person and nature, I'm not saying that "person" is an additional aspect of human nature. Rather, as Michael Wilkinson explains, a person is *who* we are. A nature is *what* we are. Every human person has a fully human nature. A human nature cannot exist without a person. That's true of Jesus Christ, *the Man*, and it's true of every *merely* human being.[2]

As Wilkinson explains, a person, every person, is the who, or "I," that acts. So when the Man Jesus acts, the Son of God is acting because he is one person. "All the person does is done through the

1. Earlier, the Nicene Creed recognized God is three persons—Father, Son, and Spirit—in one nature/essence.

2. Wilkinson, *Crowned with Glory and Honor*, 295–96.

nature, and all that happens to the nature happens to the person."[3] When the human nature of Jesus (body and soul) was crucified, the person Jesus (God the Son) was crucified. And when Jesus acted, he did so as man, one of us. That means that when Jesus ascended, one of us, a Man, the perfect Man, is now in heaven for us as our Mediator (1 John 2:1–2).

For everyone trusting in Jesus Christ as Lord, this means we have access to God through the one Mediator, the Man Christ Jesus (1 Tim 2:5). Therefore, the author of Hebrews exhorts us, "Since then we have a great high priest who has passed through the heavens, Jesus, the Son of God, let us hold fast our confession. For we do not have a high priest who is unable to sympathize with our weaknesses, but one who in every respect has been tempted as we are, yet without sin. Let us then with confidence draw near to the throne of grace, that we may receive mercy and find grace to help in time of need" (Heb 4:14–16). This passage is a great encouragement to persevere in faith and to seek God in prayer—something no animal or machine can do. And when you pray, you, a person, are praying, communing with God. You can say, "I am praying."

This person-in-nature reality helps explain how Jesus Christ can save us. He is fully human in nature, so Jesus can die for our sins in our place—a sinless, perfectly obedient human dying in the place of sinful humans. He took our guilt and died as our Representative-Substitute, so God can forgive us the guilt for our sin. He also perfectly obeyed as a *person-through-nature* (a person acting through his human nature) so that his obedience can be credited to sinful (but forgiven) humans as perfect obedience. Though we human persons rebelled against God ("I" sinned, not human nature), God can forgive us and count us as righteous ("I" am forgiven and counted righteous, not human nature).[4]

3. Wilkinson, *Crowned with Glory and Honor*, 296.

4. I will address our sinful nature in chapter 8.

RESPONSIBILITIES AND RELATIONSHIPS

Recognizing every human is a person, not merely body and soul but a body-soul person, has implications for the pressing ethical and practical questions we face today. For example, the baby in a womb, from the moment of conception, is a unique person, distinct from the mother, even as he or she inhabits the mother's womb. Therefore, abortion is never right, for it is an attack on an image bearer, a person, not a removal of some unwanted tissue, like cancer.[5] Likewise, a dead body is still to be treated with respect and honor because that body still belongs to a person. Recognizing that every human is a person guarantees rights but also means we are responsible for him/her (as we saw in chapter 3).

Understanding that we are human persons has implications for responsibility. I am responsible for my actions. I cannot blame others for what I think, say, or do. We can only uphold justice by recognizing that we are moral, volitional (willing, deciding, choosing) persons. And even persons who are incapable of willful actions (such as someone who has mental developmental disorders or diseases or who has become incapacitated) is still a human person toward whom we are to care for responsibly.

We, as persons, are to draw near to God to "offer to God acceptable worship, with reverence and awe" (Heb 12:28). Because we are persons with human natures, if the soul (one part of our nature) continues after death, I, the person, continue and will worship God even as I await the final resurrection. This makes sense of why, in Revelation 6, we read, "When he [Jesus] opened the fifth seal, I saw under the altar the souls of those who had been slain for the word of God and for the witness they had borne. They cried out with a loud voice, 'O Sovereign Lord, holy and true, how long before you will judge and avenge our blood on those who dwell on the earth?'" (Rev 6:9–10). Notice, these are "the souls *of those* [persons] *who* had been slain" for following Jesus. It is *their* blood, from their physical bodies, that was shed. The body and soul may

5. I am not addressing the rare, delicate, and very difficult decisions that have to be made to save a mother's life.

have been separated by death, but the person continues after death because he/she is united to the living Lord Jesus. We do not enter some person-less nirvana or face reincarnation into another form. Instead, "it is appointed for man to die once, and after that comes judgment" (Heb 9:27). Every person will stand before God in judgment, whether great or seemingly insignificant in this life, to give account because we are willing, acting agents (Rev 20:12–13).

Understanding that every person is created in the image and likeness of God also has implications for our responsibility toward him/her and guides how we speak of that person and treat him/her. Diseases and sins do not define people. A Christian who struggles with alcohol is not first and foremost an alcoholic but a Christian. As hard as it can be, we must be careful how we speak because our words can have the power of life and death, of hope and freedom, because either our words come from the truth or our words may only pile on more reasons for shame and despair (Prov 18:21, John 8:31–32). This is true for persons struggling with despair or depression, anger, anxiety, etc. Likewise, as John Dunlop points out, we should not think of persons with dementia (or other cognitive diseases and disorders) as being defined by the dementia. Rather, he/she is a person with dementia.[6] We should thus treat people with dementia, or other such diseases, with respect and dignity even as their cognitive abilities decline because they are persons created in God's image and likeness.[7] Visiting and caring for such persons is an act of love toward God and neighbor, especially when done in the name of Jesus (Matt 25:31–46).

But not only does a proper understanding of humans as persons determine our responsibility toward them; it also impacts our relationships with them. I specifically want to address a very recent problem regarding relationships: smart phones, AI, and social media. I remember a time when I had to make collect calls to ask my parents to pick me up from school. I was getting my undergraduate degree when I got my first cell phone. Later, I got a flip phone. And I was working on my master's degree when I got a Facebook

6. Dunlop, *Finding Grace*, 12.

7. Dunlop, *Finding Grace*, 17.

account. Today, I have a smart phone and regularly speak with people who are skilled at using AI. We have come a long way.

All of these technological advances have not come without a cost, however. In his book *The Anxious Generation*, Jonathan Haidt (who is not a Christian, as of this publication), details the extremely detrimental effects of smart phones and social media on children and youth. He notes four features that have changed in social interactions (relationships) due to the use of smart phones and social media, especially on children and youth. Social interactions are now "disembodied" rather than "embodied"; they no longer happen at the same time "with subtle cues about timing and turn taking," such as talking with one another face-to-face, but happen at differing times through texts and comments; the interactions can be many at one time rather than one interaction at a time; and rather than requiring deep investment in the relationships, relationships and communities tend to be "short-lived" and "disposable."[8] Virtual relationships are no substitute for genuine personal relationships. And constantly seeing highly curated content on social media posts tempts a person to covet what someone else has or the apparent success of others' lives, contributing to anxiety and depression. Since humans are persons, such impersonal interactions, if not balanced by many other personal interactions, can and will be detrimental and dehumanizing.

As Christians, we should recognize the harm such impersonal interactions can have, because humans are persons in a body-soul nature. Such technologies can addict and enslave us, and yet, we may have the illusion that we're building relationships and in control. AI that can now mimic human interactions can have the same results. Yet no matter what AI can do, an AI chatbot is not and will never be a human person because it's not made in God's image. God did not design us to be ruled by technology but to exercise dominion over it with self-control. Real relationships with other human persons are essential for every person to thrive, and they are a gift of God, no matter how difficult such relationships may be.

8. Haidt, *Anxious Generation*, 9–10.

As we consider how God has made us in his image, human persons, the right response is worship. David responds in Psalm 139:14, "I praise you, for I am fearfully and wonderfully made. Wonderful are your works; my soul [i.e., "I"] knows it very well." Your right response, as a human person, is to worship the God who designed you, fashioned you, and sustains you by his providential care. And if you are redeemed, you have an even greater reason to worship the Lord.

5

Body and Soul

WHAT IF SOMEONE ASKS you, "What makes up humans? What is the 'stuff' of human nature?" How would you respond? According to materialists, the universe is only matter and energy, so humans are only body, like everything in the universe (they say). Ancient Gnosticism (and Christian Science) said that matter is evil, and the immaterial part of our being (soul) is what's truly important. These differing non-Christian worldviews come to very differing conclusions about what makes up humans.

According to Scripture, humans are made up of both material and immaterial aspects of our nature. Genesis 2:7 says, "Then the LORD God formed the man of dust from the ground and breathed into his nostrils the breath of life, and the man became a living creature." Adam, the first man, was made of dust—a material aspect of his nature. So we are created of flesh and blood. But Adam only became a living creature when God breathed into his nostrils the breath of life—an immaterial aspect of his nature. So we are also soul, or spirit. And both body and soul are good aspects of God's very good creation (Gen 1:31).

As Craig Troxel writes, "God made man as a unified integrity of body and soul." He continues, "Together [body and soul] form an organic psychosomatic (body-soul) unity, or what is also called *holistic dualism*."[1] The Bible consistently teaches that humans are both material and immaterial. The immaterial is sometimes termed *heart*, *soul*, *mind*, *spirit*, or *inner man*. Whichever term is used to describe the metaphysical aspect of humans, each person is material and immaterial, body and soul.

The Bible presents humans as a body-soul unity but also presents body and soul as distinct from one another. As J. Gresham Machen writes, "The Bible does teach that the soul is a substance [though nonphysical] distinct from the body, and that it may exist, and in the case of those who die before the return of Christ and the last judgment, actually does exist, separate from the body," even though the separation of the body and soul is not natural or desirable.[2] First Corinthians 15:20–23 teaches that Christians aren't looking forward to a disembodied state but the resurrection of the dead (see John 5:25–29, 1 Thess 4:13–18). Jesus rose bodily, and we will be raised bodily like him.

TWO PARTS OR THREE?

Christians have debated whether humans are two parts (body and soul, called *dichotomy*) or whether humans are three parts (body, soul, and spirit, called *trichotomy*). Both views agree that the terms for soul and spirit are generally used interchangeably in Scripture, but trichotomists believe the soul and spirit are different and distinct immaterial aspects of every person.

Trichotomists believe that having three aspects reflects the Triune nature of God (since humans are created in God's image). Sometimes trichotomists claim that it is the spirit of the person that is dead in sin, not the body or soul, and it's the spirit that must be renewed by the Holy Spirit of God. To support their view, trichotomists often appeal to Hebrews 4:12, which states, "For the word of God is living and active, sharper than any two-edged sword, piercing to the division of soul and of spirit, of joints and of

1. Troxel, *What Is Man?*, 12; emphasis original.
2. Machen, *Christian View of Man*, 126.

marrow, and discerning the thoughts and intentions of the heart." They also appeal to 1 Thessalonians 5:23: "Now may the God of peace himself sanctify you completely, and may your whole spirit and soul and body be kept blameless at the coming of our Lord Jesus Christ." These two texts speak of the body, soul, and spirit and seem to indicate a distinction between soul and spirit (at least on the surface).

In response, dichotomists claim that there's no reason for the human nature to reflect the triunity of God since God is one in essence but three persons. Since God is not three in nature (essence) but three in person, the trichotomist position that human nature reflects divine persons is a logical error. There is also no biblical warrant for claiming that only the spirit of the person is dead in sin. Scripture testifies the whole person is dead in sin and corrupt (Eph 2:1–3). While mature Christians may make this error, it is a serious error. As Machen says (and it's worth quoting him in whole),

> It [this view of the spirit alone being dead in sin] encourages what may be called an "empty-room" view of the presence of God in the redeemed man—the notion that before a man becomes a Christian he is pretty much all right except that there is one room in him that is vacant, the room that ought to be a temple of God. It encourages, in other words, the notion that what happens when a man becomes a Christian is merely that one part of the man's nature, the "spiritual" part, a part previously neglected, is developed and given the place which it ought to have in human life.
>
> Such a notion fails to do justice to the teachings of the Bible. The real state of human nature after the fall of man is not that one part of it has been cut off or can attain only a stunted growth, but that all of it is corrupt. The real thing that happens when a man becomes a Christian is not that God is set up and enthroned in a part of man's nature which before was like an empty room, but that the whole man, corrupt before because of sin, is transformed by the regenerating power of the Spirit of God.[3]

3. Machen, *Christian View of Man*, 144.

The Christian is already regenerate by God, but this work is not yet complete, as we await the return of Christ and final restoration of the whole person, including the body (Rom 8:18–25).

The texts of 1 Thessalonians and Hebrews may best be explained by the truth that the Bible regularly refers to differing aspects of the immaterial person. For instance, Jesus commands to love the Lord your God with all your heart, soul, mind, and strength (Mark 12:30). Jesus isn't saying that heart, soul, and mind are all different immaterial aspects but is calling for complete devotion to God. "Surely the point is not that the heart, soul, and mind compose separate entities of human nature. Rather, they are ideas that overlap."[4] Scripture often refers to "body and soul" or "body and spirit" in interchangeable ways (see Matt 10:28 and 1 Cor 7:34).[5] For these reasons, it is best to understand humans as holistic, body-soul unities.

CARING FOR BODY AND SOUL

While for the above reasons I believe the dichotomist understanding of human nature is the teaching of the Bible, either way, as Christians we must recognize that body and soul (the whole of human nature) were created good and are important. When Paul says that bodily discipline is of some benefit, his point wasn't to say that the body isn't very important but the soul is. Rather, Paul's encouraging Timothy to pursue godliness in all of life because godliness is beneficial in this life and the next—rather than observing Jewish myths (Paul's not even referring to physical exercise as we practice it today; 1 Tim 4:7–8). Our physical bodies are, in this life, wearing out as we age, but the body is still the temple of God's Spirit and to be nourished and cared for (1 Cor 6:19, 2 Cor 5:1–5). Exercise and good nutrition are important. But neither are we to be materialists who, in vanity, spend an inordinate amount of time body-sculpting to the neglect of other areas of life.

4. Troxel, *What Is Man?*, 15.

5. For further study, see Hoekema, *Created in God's Image*, 204–10.

We see the goodness of our physical bodies both in the truth that God created us physical beings and in that Jesus became a physical Man to save us (he took on body and soul).

> Since therefore the children share in flesh and blood, he himself likewise partook of the same things, that through death he might destroy the one who has the power of death, that is, the devil, and deliver all those who through fear of death were subject to lifelong slavery. For surely it is not angels that he helps, but he helps the offspring of Abraham. Therefore he had to be made like his brothers in every respect, so that he might become a merciful and faithful high priest in the service of God, to make propitiation for the sins of the people. (Heb 2:14–17)

Jesus became like us in every respect to save us entirely. Self-harm, whether physical mutilation like cutting or removing unwanted physical features or suppressing unwanted hormones such as in "gender reassignment surgery," may be acceptable in a form of Gnosticism that teaches the body either doesn't matter or is evil. Such false teaching, however, denies the goodness of God creating persons as body-soul unities. Such willful harm done to the body will likewise harm the soul. This is also the reason why we cannot willfully harm the bodies of other persons (whether through rape or other forms of sexual or physical abuse). We also must take care not to sin against them in the words we speak (see Eph 4:29). Jesus came to save persons, body and soul, so we must care for body and soul.[6] Materialistic, secular methods for treating the body (or even the physical brain) without any concern for the soul are insufficient and ultimately harmful to the person being treated.

God wisely created both physical and spiritual beings. God likes physical things; that's why he made a physical creation with physical humans. So we should worship him as physical beings and should thank and praise him for his wise design. "You were bought with a price. So glorify God *in your body*" (1 Cor 6:20;

6. I will not be able to address the practice of biblical counseling, but this is surely reason for affirming the need of biblical counseling as much as it affirms the need for good physicians.

emphasis mine). As we consider that human nature includes both body and soul, it's important to consider that God created us male and female for his glory. We will explore this (now controversial) truth in the next chapter.

6

Male and Female

WHAT SEEMED SO OBVIOUS is now questioned and rejected. Throughout American history, no one would have thought twice about how many genders exist or what those genders are. But today, people cannot agree on *how many* genders there are, let alone *what* those genders are. Some sources today say sixty-eight genders exist, while others claim seventy-two. Even Wikipedia doesn't quite have the answer. Under the topic "List of Gender Identities," Wikipedia states, "This is a dynamic list and may never be able to satisfy particular standards for completeness. . . . This is a list of gender identities. Gender identity can be understood to include how people describe, present, and feel about themselves."[1] With such uncertainty and disagreement, the only thing that's certain is that the list of possible genders will continue to increase and confusion will continue to abound.

In stark contrast, the Bible clearly states that God created two sexes, two genders. "God created man in his own image, in the image of God he created him; male and female he created them" (Gen 1:27). Since mankind is created by God, God alone has the right to define human sexuality and gender. Gender is not merely a social construct but part of the goodness of God's creation, even though

1. Wikipedia, "List of Gender Identities," para. 1.

differing cultures may have some differing ways that men express their masculinity and women express their femininity.

Why did God create humans male and female, and why is this important? In Genesis 1:26–28, it's clear that God created mankind as male and female to fulfill his creation mandate to "multiply and fill the earth and subdue it" (Gen 1:28). Mankind could only multiply and fill the earth with image bearers through procreation. And only through multiplying to fill the earth could mankind exercise dominion over God's world. God created us male and female to fulfill his good purpose for us.

The Bible is clear that all humans, male and female, are created in God's image and likeness. Men and women are equally image bearers. That's why Adam sings (or waxes poetic) when he first sees Eve: "This at last is bone of my bones and flesh of my flesh; she shall be called Woman, because she was taken out of Man" (Gen 2:23). God didn't create any of the animals in his image and likeness. As a relational being, Adam needed a suitable helper to be his partner and companion, and no animal could do. Though God consistently declared his creation "good," the only time God says, "It is not good," is when the man is alone, because he cannot fulfill his purpose and responsibility or have relationship with one like him. So God fashioned the woman to be his partner (Gen 2:18–20).

God took the woman from the man's side for at least two reasons. First, so that she would be the man's equal. Puritan commentator Matthew Henry captures this thought well and poetically when he says, she was "not made out of his head to rule over him, nor out of his feet to be trampled upon by him, but out of his side to be equal with him, under his arm to be protected, and near his heart to be beloved."[2] Second, she's taken from man because the man is to be the leader in the relationship. He was the one to whom God gave the command and expected him to communicate God's expectations to the woman (Gen 2:16–17). Likewise, we see the order of the relationships of Adam and Eve in that God created Adam first, Adam named Eve, and Eve is created to be Adam's

2. Henry, *Genesis to Deuteronomy*, 20.

helper, not vice versa (Gen 2:18). The apostle Paul later grounded commands for church leadership in God's order of creation (1 Tim 2:13). Furthermore, Paul expected and commanded husbands and fathers to take the lead in their families to fulfill God's created design and purpose in an orderly way (Eph 5:25; 6:4).

That God created humans male and female has many implications for today. First, there's a goodness to both men and women as image bearers. Men and women, boys and girls, are equal in personhood and importance. Male and female persons are equally important and equally valuable to God.[3] In union with Christ, "there is neither male nor female" because all are one in Christ (Gal 3:28). But there is also a goodness to the differences and distinctions between men and women. Those complementary differences are one good aspect of God's wise creation, and such differences and distinctions are not removed in redemption. If we do not recognize and honor the distinctions between male and female, we do so to our own peril and the peril of our society.[4]

Today we face many challenges to God's good design of humans as male and female. Yet our contemporary challenges to the fact that God created humans male and female are not new. The church has faced similar challenges to those we are facing today. According to the Gnostics, early heretics who combined Greek philosophy with Christianity, deliverance came through overcoming the male and female distinctions and differences. The Gospel of Thomas says, "When you make the two into one, and when you make the inner as the outer, and the upper as the lower, and when

3. Grudem, *Systematic Theology*, 456.

4. The preamble to the Nashville Statement on biblical manhood and womanhood rightly states, "By and large the spirit of our age no longer discerns or delights in the beauty of God's design for human life. Many deny that God created human beings for his glory, and that his good purposes for us include our personal and physical design as male and female. It is common to think that human identity as male and female is not part of God's beautiful plan, but is, rather, an expression of an individual's autonomous preferences. The pathway to full and lasting joy through God's good design for his creatures is thus replaced by the path of shortsighted alternatives that, sooner or later, ruin human life and dishonor God" (The Council on Biblical Manhood and Womanhood, "Nashville Statement," para. 1).

you make male and female into a single one, so that the male shall not be male, and the female shall not be female: . . . then you will enter [the kingdom]."[5]

The thought process undergirding the "Transgender Revolution" of today is very similar to ancient Gnosticism. The revolutionaries today believe personal freedom is to be found in overcoming the physical reality (male and female) to be who you feel you truly are. Such thinking denies the goodness of the material world God created. It also harms those who take part in this lie, only adding to their confusion and damaging and deforming the body (if physical or chemical attempts are made to alter the body).[6] If a person has a biologically male body, God has designed that person to be male (and vice versa), even if his mind wrongly believes he is actually a woman, because God designed him to be a male.[7]

The goodness of God's complementary design for humans is also seen in the unique roles God assigns to men and women. In Genesis 2:4–17, God created man to spread his purposes throughout the world, to live in an obedient relationship with God in God's presence, and to work and keep, serve and protect, in dependence on God, rather than self-reliance. Genesis 2:15 states, "The LORD God took the man and put him in the garden of Eden to work it and keep it." Later, these same words were used to describe how Israel was to obey God and guard against false teaching: "You shall walk after the LORD your God and fear him and *keep* his commandments and obey his voice, and you shall *serve* him and hold fast to him" (Deut 13:4; emphasis mine).

Adam was a priest-king, serving and guarding as the Levites and priests were to serve and protect the sanctity of God's tabernacle and temple. As with Adam, all men are created to be proactive and intentional. Men are created to work, to serve others as

5. Saying 22, as quoted in Merillat, "When the Two Become One," para. 3; brackets original. For a deeper consideration of the similarities between Gnosticism and the current transgender revolution, see Fairbairn, "Theological Anthropology."

6. For further study on gender and sexuality, see Ligonier Ministries, *Field Guide.*

7. Burk et al., *Male and Female*, 70.

an outflow of God's love to neighbor. Through work, men provide and can share (Eph 4:28). God created men strong to sacrificially serve and protect others, especially those who are vulnerable. While such truths have been challenged and tend to be rejected as backward or old fashioned today, there is a dignity to men when they live according to God's word consistently, and it is genuinely beautiful and good, for it is God's design. Male headship is good, though it has certainly seen abuses throughout human history.

God created women as helpers for building and nurturing relationships. Women are adequate, or fit, helpers for men. That is, a woman's unique disposition is complementary to that of men (Gen 2:18). This help occurs within a relationship, especially within a covenant relationship, because God created a man and woman to be joined in the covenant of marriage (Gen 2:24–25). A helper is not someone who is lesser than another person but a person who has a specific, indispensable role.[8] A wife is to submit to her own husband, not to every man, because the husband is the leader in the home and has final responsibility before God, not because he is better in any way (Eph 5:22–24). This created order of persons in the marriage relationship reflects the relationships of the Triune God.[9]

As Ligon Duncan and Susan Hunt explain, to be a helper is to be strong, compassionate, community building, and a life giver. The opposite of being a helper is to hinder and be a life taker, which is what happens when men and women compete in their roles rather than complementing each other (Gen 3:16).[10] "There is nothing more beautiful, satisfying, delightful, and God-glorifying than when men and women live and work together in

8. Mathews, *Genesis 1:1—11:26*, 213–14. God himself is regularly described by the same Hebrew term translated,"helper" to his covenant partner. In Exodus 18:4 God as Helper defends. In Psalm 20:2, as Helper, God supports. In Psalm 33:20, as Helper, God shields and protects. In Psalm 70:5, as Helper, God delivers from distress. In Psalm 72:12–14, as Helper, God rescues the poor and needy. In Psalm 86:17, as Helper, God comforts.

9. Grudem, *Systematic Theology*, 459–60.

10. Duncan and Hunt, *Women's Ministry*, 35.

complementarity."[11] This is God's wise and good design, and it is right and beautiful and supports human flourishing.

God established the relationship of husband and wife ultimately to point to the relationship of Jesus Christ and his bride, the church (Eph 5:25–31). Jesus loves the church and demonstrated his love by sacrificing himself for the life and flourishing of his church. He is the true and complete pattern for the sacrificial leadership of a man in his family (Mark 10:42–45). The proper response to God's revealed mystery is to stand amazed and worship God for the beauty and wisdom of his design. In the next chapter, we will consider marriage and singleness in greater depth.

11. Duncan and Hunt, *Women's Ministry*, 33.

7

Singleness, Marriage, and Children

"I LOVE YOU. YOU complete me."[1] While Tom Cruise's words as his character Jerry Maguire are romantic, such sentiments can cause great confusion. If a woman truly "completes" a man (or vice versa), does that mean he/she is less than fully human while single? Does that mean that only people who are in the one-flesh union of marriage are complete divine image bearers? Are single people somehow deficient human beings? What about divorcees and widows and widowers? And how do children fit into God's plans for humanity?

SINGLENESS

We must again turn to Scripture for the answers. And the place to begin is with the true Man, Jesus Christ. Jesus lived about thirty-three years as a single man. Was Jesus less than human? Of course not. That's ludicrous! When God the Son became man, he was fully human from the moment of conception in Mary's womb (see Luke 1:39–44). Yes, Jesus grew as every human does, but he didn't become more human. From conception, Jesus was made human in every way so that he might save us (Heb 2:14–17). Though he was

1. Crowe, *Jerry Maguire*, 2:09:47.

never married, Jesus wasn't deficient. He is "the image of God" in his person (Col 1:15, Heb 1:2–3). Jesus doesn't only become complete man when he and the church (his bride) are joined forever (Rev 19).

Likewise, the apostle Paul was apparently single throughout his life (this seems to be what he calls his "gift" in 1 Cor 7:6–7). This means that singleness is an acceptable lifestyle. People who remain single, whether by choice or through the circumstances of life, are not less human than married couples (see Matt 19:10–12). Rather, single persons can devote themselves to God with undivided commitment (1 Cor 7:32–35). When God said, "It is not good that the man should be alone" in Genesis 2:18, he wasn't saying that Adam was not fully human until God made Eve. Rather, Adam could not have relationships with other humans without the woman. Single people need relationships with other people as much as married people do. But more to the point, Adam was incapable of being fruitful and multiplying to fill the earth with image bearers without a suitable helper. He could not fulfill his role and responsibilities alone. Likewise, single persons are to be fruitful and multiply to fill the earth with image bearers in a similar way to married persons. Like married persons, single persons are to refrain from sexual relations outside of the marriage covenant, but those who are single can make disciples of Jesus, image bearers in the likeness of Jesus who will populate the new earth (Rom 8:29, Eph 5:1–2).

MARRIAGE

Though marriage rates have dropped in America due to the social acceptability of sex outside of marriage, many people will still get married. According to God's original intention, "therefore a man shall leave his father and his mother and hold fast to his wife, and they shall become one flesh. And the man and his wife were both naked and were not ashamed" (Gen 2:24–25). As Jesus confirms, God's creational intention for marriage has not changed. Jesus confronted the leaders of his day, many of whom accepted a liberal practice of divorce: "Have you not read that he who created them from the beginning made them male and female, and said, 'Therefore a man shall leave his father and his mother and hold fast to his wife, and the two shall become one flesh'? So they are no longer two but one flesh. What therefore God has joined together, let not man separate" (Matt 19:4–6). God designed marriage to be a lifelong covenant between one man and one woman.

What Genesis and Jesus say runs counter to the cultural understanding and practices of marriage today. The practice of easy, no-fault divorce is clearly unbiblical. The Bible puts clear restrictions on divorce. While there's some disagreement among Christians as to specifics (or if the Bible permits divorce at all), the Bible never commands or commends divorce. Instead, Jesus limits divorce to infidelity alone (Matt 19:7–9). Paul likewise expects marriage to be for a lifetime, even if a believer is married to an unbelieving spouse (1 Cor 7:12–14). The only other reason God permits a believer to divorce an unbelieving spouse is "if the unbelieving partner separates, let it be so. In such cases the brother or sister is not enslaved. God has called you to peace" (1 Cor 7:15). Only in such cases is the offended party then allowed to remarry.

God's original intention likewise prohibits any polygamous or polyamorous relationships. As our society has redefined marriage, the discussion surrounding polyamory (multiple intimate relationships) and polygamy (multiple marriage partners) has again entered public discussion. Persons throughout the Bible, including Abraham, Jacob, David, and Solomon, had multiple wives and/or concubines. Though such practices were culturally acceptable, they violated God's clear intentions set forth in Genesis 2 and reaffirmed by Jesus. Sex outside of marriage in any form (including lust in any form, such as the use of pornography) likewise violates the one-flesh covenant union of marriage God designed (Matt 5:27–29). Interestingly, the first example of polygamy in the Bible was by a man known for his utter wickedness: Lamech (Gen 4:19–24). According to God's design and intentions, only "the two" become one flesh.

The attempt to redefine marriage in unbiblical ways has become absurd. The *Obergefell* decision by the Supreme Court may have legalized same-sex marriage throughout the United States, but it did not change God's biblical standards. Instead, as Jesus says, God originally created humans male and female for one man and one woman to be married. Any other union not only goes against God's intention and law, but such unions are signs of the wrath of God that gives people over to sin and its consequences for rejecting him and his ways (Rom 1:26–27).

Recently, sologamy or autogamy—marrying oneself—has gained popularity. While this is certainly preposterous, as it goes against the very idea of a covenant (which requires two parties), supporters have attempted to argue that "it affirms one's value and leads to a happier life."[2] But since God has authority over humanity, declaring it is not good for the man to be alone, and he designed marriage as the covenant of one man and one woman, self-marriage clearly violates God's design and is nonsensical.

Perhaps worst of all, every corruption of marriage is a denial of the gospel of Jesus Christ. The marital union of a man and a woman pictures God's relationship with his people (see Hos 1) and is a picture of the union of Jesus Christ and his bride, the church. In Ephesians 5:31–32, the apostle Paul reaches back to Genesis 2 and says, "'Therefore a man shall leave his father and mother and hold fast to his wife, and the two shall become one flesh.' This mystery is profound, and I am saying that it refers to Christ and the church." Every marriage of a man and woman, even unbelievers, is a picture of the union of Jesus Christ and his church. Every such wedding is a foreshadow of the marriage supper of Jesus and his bride (Rev 19:9–10).

Because marriage pictures and proclaims the gospel, God gives explicit commands about how husbands and wives are to conduct themselves in marriage. According to Ephesians 5:25–30,

> Husbands, love your wives, as Christ loved the church and gave himself up for her, that he might sanctify her, having cleansed her by the washing of water with the word, so that he might present the church to himself in splendor, without spot or wrinkle or any such thing, that

2. Wikipedia, "Sologamy," para. 1.

> she might be holy and without blemish. In the same way husbands should love their wives as their own bodies. He who loves his wife loves himself. For no one ever hated his own flesh, but nourishes and cherishes it, just as Christ does the church, because we are members of his body.

God likewise commands wives, "Wives, submit to your own husbands, as to the Lord. For the husband is the head of the wife even as Christ is the head of the church, his body, and is himself its Savior. Now as the church submits to Christ, so also wives should submit in everything to their husbands" (Eph 5:22–24). While these commands are countercultural, and even despised today, they are the only way for a husband and wife to experience God's blessing in their union (see 1 Pet 3:1–7).

Our society is experiencing an epidemic regarding domestic abuse and sexual abuse. The answer isn't to jettison Christian teachings and practices of marriage or the unique roles of men and women. Instead, biblical Christianity is the only true solution to abuse in all its forms. Domestic and sexual abuses are clear violations of the personhood and nature of human beings and are forms of unrighteousness (sin) by the perpetrator and injustice toward the victim (whether male or female). Furthermore, domestic and sexual abuse violate God's design for the covenant of marriage. A man or woman who abuses his/her spouse has transgressed the one-flesh union of the covenant by failing to love the other partner (see Eph 5:28–29). Furthermore, any form of sexual abuse transgresses the one-flesh union of marriage. A biblical view of humans and marriage is essential to combatting sexual and domestic abuse. And local churches and Christians are right to protect, support, and help those who are victims of such abuse.[3]

3. For a further scholarly study on marriage, see Kostenberger and Jones, *God, Marriage, and Family*. For biblical answers to questions on marriage, see Newheiser, *Marriage, Divorce, and Remarriage*.

CHILDREN

Many societies are facing what some have termed a "baby bust." Many European nations, the United States, Japan, China, and other societies are experiencing rapidly decreasing birth rates as many people either choose to not have children or delay having children until they get older.[4] This declining birth rate is likely tied to falling marriage rates and the increasing age for first marriages, as so-called "traditional marriage" is no longer valued in many societies, though other reasons also contribute (such as China's historic one-child policy).

As Christians, we recognize the goodness of children, as God commanded humans to "be fruitful and multiply" to fill the earth with image bearers (Gen 1:28). Children are a blessing from God (Ps 127:3–5). Though secular society may put forth reasons for encouraging higher birth rates, such as economic growth or having citizens for the work force and military, as Christians, we must recognize God's good purposes of marriage, family, and children are inextricably connected. There is a biblical, creational order: first marriage, then children (rather than procreation outside of marriage). We must model and defend God's design, recognizing that it is not only good for society and the world, but it is ultimately for God's glory.

While much more could be said about singleness, marriage, and the family, the Bible clearly presents singleness as acceptable for God's people. Single persons are fully human persons who can fulfill God's purposes for them.[5] Marriage is a way to fulfill God's purposes in the calling of husband and wife, and God designed this union not only for intimacy (relational and sexual) and procreation but also to be a picture of the gospel. Even before sin entered the world, God designed marriage to point to the union of Jesus

4. Though it is a very important subject, I will not be able to address in vitro fertilization (IVF) here. However, the destruction of frozen embryos is the destruction of human persons since even outside of the womb a human person is a human person.

5. For further study on singleness, see Danylak, *Singleness in God's Redemptive Story*.

and the church. The only right response to such depths of wisdom is to worship God, whether in singleness or marriage. And yet, as with every other aspect of humanity, marriage has been corrupted by sin. It is to the reality of sin that we must turn.

8

The Fall and Sin

My family and I lived in Wisconsin for nine years. While living there, I regularly saw a bumper sticker that read, "I put the sin in Wisconsin." While I never owned the bumper sticker, I could have. Everyone living in Wisconsin could slap that bumper sticker onto their car because every human being who has ever existed (except Jesus of Nazareth) is a sinner. What is sin, and how has it impacted mankind?

According to Genesis 3, sin entered the world in what we call *the fall*. When God created man, he gave him the command to not eat from the tree of the knowledge of good and evil. God warned Adam that if he ate of the tree, he would surely die as the consequence for his disobedience (Gen 2:17). Although God created mankind in a state of innocence as a part of his very good creation, sin entered the world through Adam and Eve's rebellion against God, the Creator. The first two humans believed the lies of the evil one rather than God's word, so they disobeyed God's clear command (Gen 3:1–6).

The serpent, Satan, tempted Adam and Eve by challenging God's word and authority. He promised them autonomy, self-rule, instead of being creatures living under God's rule. Satan, the accuser, cast doubt on God's goodness by intentionally twisting God's command so that it sounded excessively limiting. He asked, "Did

God actually say, 'You shall not eat of any tree in the garden'?" (Gen 3:2). While the woman corrected the serpent and noted that eating from the forbidden tree brought the penalty of death (though she did add restriction to God's command), the serpent then accused God of lying and selfish intentions. "You will not surely die. For God knows that when you eat of it your eyes will be opened and you will be like God, knowing good and evil" (Gen 3:4–5). The serpent cleverly cast doubt on God's word and made God's word a debatable matter. And who would trust the word of someone who just wants to keep them down?

Furthermore, we see Satan's craftiness in subverting God's created order by approaching and tempting the woman rather than the man (see 1 Tim 2:13–14). Satan not only tempted them to reject God's authority, he also gave an example of how to go around those in authority. Now, this in no way excuses Adam. The text is clear that Adam was "with her," and he failed to lead and guard his wife by cleansing the garden of the evil serpent. Instead, Adam listened to the voice of his wife rather than the word of God and ate the fruit when she offered it to him (Gen 3:6).

The consequences of their sin were immediate: "Then the eyes of both were opened, and they knew that they were naked" (Gen 3:7). In fear, they vainly attempted to hide their naked guilt and shame by sewing fig leaves together for a covering. Then, they hid themselves from God, excused their own actions, and shifted blame rather than taking responsibility for what they had done (Gen 3:8–13). Their rebellion made a rift between themselves and God. God cursed the fulfillment of their roles and responsibilities, making relationships, multiplying, and having dominion over creation a battle (Gen 3:15–19).

Because Adam was the father and representative of all humanity, sin entered the world through him and spread to all humanity through him. Romans 5:12 says, "Sin came into the world through one man, and death through sin, and so death spread to all men because all sinned." In Adam, every human is guilty before God, lacks righteousness, and has a nature corrupted by sin from the womb (see Ps 51:5).[1] Since Adam was our representative and head, every human being is counted as a sinner "in Adam." Mankind is thus guilty because of Adam's sin, so death reigns over humanity as the consequence for our guilt. As the apostle Paul writes, "Many died through one man's trespass," and "One trespass led to condemnation for all men" (Rom 5:15, 18). Furthermore, all mankind lacks righteousness in our standing before God. As Romans 3:10 says, "None is righteous, no, not one."

In Adam, every human has inherited a corrupted nature. As Romans 6 sums up, humanity is enslaved to sin and under sin's terrible dominion. While every human is responsible for his/her own actions, in sin no human is truly "free" since humans are slaves to sin apart from Christ. As Craig Troxel explains, "As a covenant-breaker, [man] essentially stands in a hostile relation to God and therefore cannot please God, nor is he even interested in doing so."[2] Ephesians 2:3 sums up the condition of humanity in sin by simply stating, "We were by nature children of wrath, like the rest of mankind." This sinful corruption of our nature results in the acts of sin we commit and an inability to do what truly pleases God, because we live for ourselves rather than God's glory. "For the mind that is set on the flesh is hostile to God, for it does not submit to God's law; indeed, it cannot. Those who are in the flesh cannot please God" (Rom 8:7–8).[3]

What is sin? Wayne Grudem helpfully defines sin as "any failure to conform to the moral law of God in act, attitude, or nature."[4] Sin is both a power that corrupts and enslaves us and the thoughts, attitudes, words, and actions that we do that do not conform to God's holy standard revealed in Scripture. We are not sinners because we sin; rather, we sin because we're sinners. But

1. The Baptist Catechism says it this way: "The sinfulness of that estate whereinto man fell, consists in the guilt of Adam's first sin, the want of original righteousness, and the corruption of his whole nature, which is commonly called original sin; together with all actual transgressions which proceed from it" (Silicon Valley Reformed Baptist Church, "Baptist Catechism," Q&A 21).

2. Troxel, *What Is Man?*, 22.

3. For further study, see Grudem, *Systematic Theology*, 490–504.

4. Grudem, *Systematic Theology*, 490.

we're sinners not because we were created this way but due to humanity's rebellion against God. While this is hard to accept, it makes the gospel possible because it means God can save us from the power and penalty of sin through the work of Jesus Christ and the Holy Spirit, as we'll consider in the next chapter.

Having a proper understanding of sin keeps us from the mistake of attributing evil to something inherent in being human. For example, as J. Gresham Machen explains, sin is not "the triumph of the lower part of man's nature over the higher part, that is the triumph of the appetites of the body over the human spirit," as some have thought.[5] This is similar to the error of ancient Gnosticism that taught matter is evil while soul (or spirit) is good. Such false thinking can lead to a form of asceticism that thinks denying urges, such as hunger or a desire to have sex (including within marriage), will make a person holier. But as Colossians 2:23 says, "These have indeed an appearance of wisdom in promoting self-made religion and asceticism and severity to the body, but they are of no value in stopping the indulgence of the flesh" because the "flesh" that Paul's referring to isn't the physical body but the rebellious disposition that leads each of us to disobey God (see 1 Tim 4:1–8).

Since sin is treason against our Creator, the penalty for sin is death (Rom 6:23). Humans do not die because we're physical beings or because death is a natural part of the world. Death is the result of sin. And throughout this life, sin results in misery. As Troxel explains, "The state of affairs between the Creator and his image-bearing creatures is that fallen man is currently under the wrath and curse of God and stands condemned."[6] In sin, humanity has made an awful exchange. Though God has made himself known through the general revelation of his creation, in our sinful state we "suppress the truth" about who God is for the lie of self-rule. Rather than honoring and thanking God for his goodness toward us, humanity has become "futile in their thinking, and their foolish hearts were darkened" (Rom 1:21). Sin affects every aspect

5. Machen, *Christian View of Man*, 177.

6. Troxel, *What Is Man?*, 23.

of us—our thinking, our desires, and our wills. And sin blinds us to the truth about God and ourselves. "Claiming to be wise, they became fools and exchanged the glory of the immortal God for images resembling mortal man and birds and animals and creeping things" (Rom 1:22–23).

At its core, sin is a worship problem. We worship the creation rather than God the Creator. At the top of the list of this idolatry is the worship of self. Every time we sin, we put self before God and believe we know better than God. Then, we ruinously become like what we worship. We experience the living death of sin so that we dishonor ourselves and fellow humans and approve of all sorts of wickedness because we have seared consciences and lack the courage and proper thinking that would enable us to call sin "sin" (Rom 1:24–32). Instead, we begin thinking and believing that good is evil and evil is good. This is the outcome of "the wrath of God" that is "revealed from heaven against all ungodliness and unrighteousness of men" (Rom 1:18). "As pollution sin defiles, as bondage it enslaves, as indebtedness it condemns, and as misery it makes our race unhappy. . . . Sin taints every aspect of human existence, and nothing lies outside its influence."[7]

Sin doesn't merely affect individuals but the societies that we create, develop, and inhabit. Humans murder one another, steal from one another, lie to one another, break their commitments to one another, abuse and rape one another, and disrespect one another. As humans form societies, wickedness becomes systemic so that societies and governments commit, allow, and celebrate racism, genocide, classism, abortion, greed, euthanasia, homosexuality, transgenderism, and a whole host of evils beyond reckoning. The result of sin is suffering, destruction, disease, rejection, and oppression on levels and to degrees beyond what any one of us can imagine or could tolerate to consider. But it is all known to the God who will judge us (Heb 4:13).

The outcome of sin is death—death for individuals and death for the beastly societies that rise and fall throughout human history (see Dan 7:1–8). Death has been the constant companion of

7. Troxel, *What Is Man?*, 23.

humanity since the fall. The refrain of the fifth chapter of the Bible is simple: "And he died." Death steals away its victims, whether one by one or *en masse*. We all face our own mortality, even as we suffer the loss of loved ones. "If death is the culmination of this life's miseries, then it is but a mere threshold to the eternal miseries of the life to come for those cursed to endure everlasting fire" away from God and his glorious presence (see 2 Thess 1:9).[8]

As we have briefly considered sin and its consequences, it's right to long for escape, to long for deliverance. But since the problem isn't outside of us but inescapably *in us*, we cannot save ourselves. The heart of our problem is the problem of the heart (see Mark 7:14–23). There is nowhere that we can run, nowhere that we can hide. This brings us to the only solution: only God can save us from eternal darkness and death. It is into this world of darkness that the Light of life has come: Jesus Christ, our only Savior.

8. Troxel, *What Is Man?*, 26.

9

Redemption and Restoration

I'M NOT A HANDYMAN. Or at least I'm not a good handyman. I try, but in reality, I need a lot of help. When we lived in Kenosha, Wisconsin, we decided to gut and renovate our main bathroom. The bathroom was ugly, dated, and had a lot of water damage. So a friend came to help me demo it and tear everything out. After tearing out the bathtub, toilet, vanity, and the dry wall, we got to work on the floor. After taking up one layer of floor, there was another below it. I was shocked to discover they had put one layer of floor over another. We then took up that layer of floor to find out there was yet another layer below. And to my chagrin, that floor covered another layer still. By the time we got to that final layer, the smell of urine that had saturated the floor for so long around the toilet had become intolerable. I was so thrilled when we finally removed all that was polluted and disgusting.

But the job wasn't complete. It took days, in fact weeks, with the help of others, to refresh the bathroom. We put in the bathtub and shower, drywall—and painted it—the exhaust fan, the floor, the toilet, and the vanity (which I did by myself, and it even worked). With baseboards and final touches, the bathroom was complete. It was restored like new.

What is God going to do with this sinful world? One day, God is going to remove from his good creation everything that still reeks of sin. Through the refining fires of judgment, God will remove all that is polluted and disgusting—or better, evil and defiling (2 Pet 3:7, 10). But God isn't planning to move out or move humanity out. God's not planning to move us to Mars or another dimension. Rather, God is making a new heaven and new earth, in which righteousness dwells (2 Pet 3:13). God isn't making all new things; he's making all things new (Rev 21:5). God is "redeeming both his imagers and his creation."[1] And God has accomplished this redemption and is applying it for the final restoration through the work and lordship of his Son, the God-Man, Jesus Christ, and the work of his Spirit.

God saves his image bearers by sending his Son, Jesus, in the likeness of Man. Only by becoming like us in every way, except that he's without sin, can Jesus truly save us. Michael Wilkinson notes four roles Jesus fulfills as God the Son become man:

> Scripture presents four major theological identities for Jesus that entail a *sufficient ontological correspondence* between his human being and ours. He is the Christ, who accomplishes salvation as both God and man. He is *the* image of God, who perfectly reveals God's real presence on the earth as a man. He is the Redeemer of man, who actually atoned for sins as a man. And he is the representative Son of Man to whom this world is being subjected for the restoration of man's righteous rule under God.[2]

Jesus truly became One of us and one with us. That's how Jesus can be the new and better Adam to represent us and save us.

As Man, Jesus can represent us and die as Man for the sins of man. Hebrews 2:17 says, "Therefore he had to be made like his brothers in every respect, so that he might become a merciful and faithful high priest in the service of God, to make propitiation for the sins of the people." He became like us so that through his death as our substitute he could "destroy the one who has the power of death, that is, the devil, and deliver all those who through fear of death were subject to lifelong slavery" (Heb 2:14–15). The penalty

1. Ashford, *Every Square Inch*, 31.

2. Wilkinson, *Crowned with Glory and Honor*, 335; emphasis original.

for sin is death, and Jesus took that penalty in his own flesh when he died on the cross to bear God's wrath in our place (Rom 6:23). He also set us free from the enslaving power of sin (John 8:31–32, Rom 6:6).

Jesus' obedient life, death, resurrection, exaltation, and continued intercession secures every aspect of salvation for his people. Since Jesus died for our sins, there is now forgiveness through his once-for-all sacrifice (Heb 10:12–18). Through faith in Jesus, Christians are united with him. By his grace, God regenerates his people, making us "alive with Christ" when we were dead in our sins (Eph 2:4–5). Therefore, Christians are new creation now, even as we await our full and final restoration (Rom 8:23, 2 Cor 5:17). Through faith, God also justified Christians as a gift of his grace. Justification is a legal declaration in which God as Judge forgives our sins and counts us as righteous in Christ—as if we had perfectly obeyed God—because Jesus died for us (Rom 3:26, 2 Cor 5:21). "Since we have been justified by faith, we have peace with God through our Lord Jesus Christ" (Rom 5:1). That is, we're reconciled to God. "There is therefore now no condemnation for those who are in Christ" (Rom 8:1) and there is no one to condemn because Jesus, the Lord and Judge, is the one who died for us and intercedes for us (Rom 8:34).

Furthermore, in Christ, believers are adopted as God's children. Our legal status is changed so that we now have the right to call God our Father (John 1:12–13, 1 John 3:1). Christians are therefore heirs of God with Jesus Christ (Rom 8:14–17, Gal 4:4–7). As God's children, Christians have received the "Spirit of adoption as sons" so that we are set apart to God and his purposes (Rom 8:15). To be set apart to God means to be sanctified. Sanctification is first positional: we now belong to God because we were sanctified when we trusted in Jesus as Lord and Savior (1 Cor 1:2, 6:11, Heb 13:12). As those set apart, we are being sanctified progressively by God's Spirit making us into the likeness of Jesus Christ (Rom 8:29, 2 Cor 3:16–17, 1 Thess 4:3). With the enslaving power of sin broken, so that sin no longer reigns over us, and because we have been made new by the Spirit, Christians can now walk in newness of life. "God's Spirit graciously and powerfully works in believers, enabling them to oppose residual sin and walk in the ways of righteousness as a new creation, to put off the old self and put on the new self" by God's powerful work in us (Rom 6:12–14, Phil 2:12–13).[3]

Ultimately, God will bring his restoring work to completion in the believer in what is termed *glorification* (Rom 8:30). "And I am sure of this, that he who began a good work in you will bring it to completion at the day of Jesus Christ" (Phil 1:6). When Jesus returns, God will raise bodily those in union with Jesus Christ to live forever in his presence in the new heaven and new earth (Rom 8:23–24; 1 Cor 15:20–23, 42–49; 2 Pet 3:13).

But God isn't merely saving individuals; he's saving us to be a people, his church. God is reconciling us not just to himself, but he's reconciling us, all the various peoples of the world, to one another as "one new man," his church (Eph 2:15). The church thus bears the image and likeness of God in union with Jesus Christ, who is himself the head of the body and the image of God (Eph 1:22–23). The church is a family, a living temple, and a kingdom of priests who will reign with Christ (Eph 2:19–22, 1 Pet 2:5–9, Rev 5:10). Through the faithful witness of the church, God is working by his Spirit to multiply disciples, those who bear the likeness of Christ, to make a new, resurrection humanity of whom Jesus is the firstborn from the dead (Col 1:18).

This means the church has a dual role. The church is to proclaim the gospel and make disciples of all the peoples of the earth, teaching them to obey the risen Lord Jesus so that they may bear his likeness (Matt 28:18–19). With the coming of Jesus Christ, God's kingdom, his saving reign, has come (Mark 1:15). But Jesus isn't only saving people and making a church, but in his people, his church, Jesus is reigning and giving a foretaste of his coming eternal reign.

Even though corrupted by sin, God's creation is still "good," and as we await the complete restoration when Jesus returns, we're to honor God through how we exercise dominion over his creation

3. Troxel, *What Is Man?*, 29.

now. As Christians, we are "to live 'between two worlds,' recognizing God's work in the present fallen world and anticipating the full completion of his work in the new heavens and new earth."[4] As the apostle Paul says, because Jesus is risen and we will be raised, "Therefore, my beloved brothers, be steadfast, immovable, always abounding in the work of the Lord, knowing that in the Lord your labor is not in vain" (1 Cor 15:58). Jesus is Lord and claims everything as his own. He is restoring it and will one day make all things new (Rev 21:5).

As God's people, we should "proclaim the excellencies of him who called us out of darkness into his marvelous light" (1 Pet 2:9). We should sing the songs of the redeemed with joyful hearts, even though we sing in Babylon as we await the final restoration of all things, when we will sing the Lord's praises as one people forever (Pss 107:1–2; 137; Rev 7:13–14, 14:3). And yet, we must remember that worship isn't only about singing God's praises. We're to worship God in every facet of life, both private and public (Col 3:17). To say, "Jesus is Lord," means Jesus is Lord of everything and over everything, including our vocations, culture, and politics.

4. Ashford, *Every Square Inch*, 33.

10

Vocation, Culture, and Government

I AM NOW LIVING and working in Chicago, which is currently the third largest city in America. I didn't grow up in Chicago. In fact, I didn't even visit Chicago until I was a junior in college. I grew up in rural, northern Ohio. We were surrounded by soybean and corn fields. I took part in 4-H, raising goats and chickens and helping my mother plant and grow flowers and vegetables. I graduated in a class of less than one hundred students. And the high school I attended had a yearly "bring your tractor to school" day, in which I never participated (in case you're wondering). While I never intended to stay in rural Ohio, I also didn't grow up expecting to live in a major metropolitan area notorious for high taxes and, at least according to legend, allowing dead people to vote (whether that ever truly happened or not, Chicago's known for it). Chicago is, in many ways, a city that epitomizes human culture and government in opposition to the holy God of Scripture.

We now turn to consider what the Bible means when it says humanity is to exercise dominion. God commanded humans to "have dominion over the fish of the sea and over the birds of the heavens and over every living thing that moves on the earth" (Gen 1:28). While sin corrupts how we exercise dominion, and we await the return of Jesus Christ to reign with him forever in the new heaven and new earth, all humans, except those incapable due to mental or physical handicap, exercise dominion in some ways. And for Christians, we should strive to exercise dominion in accordance with our redeemed status and nature. We should pray, "Your kingdom come, your will be done, on earth as it is in heaven," and seek to be agents of seeing God's kingdom purposes accomplished not just in us as individuals or in the church but in the world (Matt 6:10).

Though we cannot possibly cover every way humans exercise dominion over God's creation, we will consider three important aspects of exercising dominion: vocation, culture, and government. Vocation refers to the callings we all have from God. Such callings could include being a son or daughter, being a student, being a husband or wife, a father or mother, a church member, a neighbor, and so on. We will consider vocation in general, but I will focus on vocation as fulfilling a calling through work. We will also consider how we all live in culture, for we all are culture-shaping persons. And finally, we will briefly consider human government. Each of these can and does have full book-length treatments. Yet it's important to understand that vocation, culture, and government are important aspects of how we function as persons created in God's image.

VOCATION

Vocation, or calling, is very broad in scope. But vocation isn't primarily about the future, such as what career you would like to have after you finish high school. Rather, vocation is primarily about what God has called you to now.[1] If you're married, God has called you to be a husband or wife. If you're a doctor, God has called you to be a doctor. God designed the world so that he often shows his love to us through the works of other people as we serve one another. While this is especially true of Christians, it is true of all humans because every person is created in the image of God.

1. Veith, *God at Work*, 57–60.

Work is one aspect of vocation. And work comes in an incomprehensible array of duties. Mothers work by changing diapers and feeding babies. Children work by doing chores and being faithful students. People work, in some sense, even in their hobbies. Planting flowers or shrubs is a form of work. Fixing your own car, or a friend's car, is work. Governing is work, and voting for those in government is a form of work. Through work we exercise "dominion" and subdue the created world. Work is one way we honor God as his image bearers (Gen 1:28).

As I was writing this chapter, I attempted to replace a leaky shower cartridge. It should have been a simple job of taking out the old cartridge and putting in the new one. But the old shower cartridge broke off, and I needed help. I contacted some Christian brothers who are more knowledgeable and skilled as handymen, but this wasn't something they had handled before. So one of them graciously contacted a plumber he knew, and the plumber came to help. I didn't stop the plumber and ask him if he was a Christian before I let him work on the problem. Rather, I recognized that, since he's a fellow human being in God's image, God has called him into this role and has skilled him for this task. Through the service of this plumber, and through the help of Christian brothers, God was showing me and my family his love so that our shower would work, and I could turn the water back on in our house before my wife and children came home.

As Gene Veith writes, "The doctrine of vocation helps Christians see the ordinary labors of life to be charged with meaning. It also helps put their work into perspective, seeing that their work is not saving them, but that they are resting in the grace of God, who in turn works through their labors to love and serve their neighbors."[2] God gave work to humans when he created the world. This may be a shock to some Christians, but work is not a result of the fall or part of the curse. Though we should take time to rest, we shouldn't work just because we have to pay bills. Rather, we work because we're created in the image of the God who works.

2. Veith, *God at Work*, 61.

"[Human] work is an imitation of God's work, a participation in God's creation and His creativity."[3]

In Colossians 3:22–25, the apostle Paul instructs servants (slaves) how to fulfill their vocation. Paul doesn't call them to revolt or engage in passive-aggressive behaviors but to serve in a manner pleasing to God: "Bondservants, obey in everything those who are your earthly masters, not by way of eye-service, as people-pleasers, but with sincerity of heart, fearing the Lord. Whatever you do, work heartily, as for the Lord and not for men, knowing that from the Lord you will receive the inheritance as your reward. You are serving the Lord Christ. For the wrongdoer will be paid back for the wrong he has done, and there is no partiality." What you do, and how you do it matters to God. Not every job is a God-honoring vocation. For example, prostitution or illegal drug dealing are not legitimate, God-honoring vocations because they are inherently sinful. But a plumber can honor God in his or her vocation the same as a pastor can. God created us to fulfill the vocations he has for us. No matter what a person does or his/her vocation, he/she is no more valuable than anyone else. Understanding humanity biblically dignifies every human being and every vocation.

CULTURE

Culture, on the other hand, isn't what any single human does but something humans do collectively. As God created us with the ability and commanded us to be fruitful and multiply and fill the earth, God's intention is for humanity to relate to one another and to the creation. When God commanded humanity collectively to have dominion, he was not calling us to rape and pillage the natural world he created. Instead, we're to rule benevolently, reflecting God's benevolent rule over us.[4] God has given us the resources we

3. Veith, *God at Work*, 62.

4. Edgar, *Created and Creating*, 167. Edgar defines cultural engagement as "the human response to the divine call to enjoy and develop the world that God has generously given to his image bearers. Culture includes the symbols,

need to develop his cosmos for human flourishing and the benefit of the entire cosmos.

Humanity in God's image is created with a God-given, God-imitating ability and desire to create cultures. As William Edgar writes, "Embedded in this human activity is (at least in germ form) the development of agriculture, the arts, economics, family dynamics, and everything that contributes to human flourishing, to the glory of God."[5] In Psalm 8, King David recognizes there is a God-ordained goodness to all of the righteous activities mankind does in fulfilling God's cultural mandate. Though humanity in sin develops sinful cultures, and though the creation is under the curse as it eagerly awaits its final freedom in the new heaven and new earth, Jesus is the Creator of all things, and he has redeemed humanity and his creation (Rom 8:19–23). Indeed, Jesus honored human culture. As Edgar explains, he "subjected himself to this world, entering a particular culture at a particular time." Jesus honored the culture in which he lived by conforming "whenever that was legitimate, to its forms and conventions."[6] And Jesus had a profound impact on his own culture and continues to impact cultures today. In the new heaven and new earth, human cultures will not cease to exist. Rather, the different cultures will bring the "glory and the honor of the nations" into God's holy city. However, nothing unclean or detestable due to sin will ever enter because it did not pass through the refining fires of judgment (Rev 21:26–27).

As God's people, we must recognize the inescapable reality of culture, even as we seek to engage in culture for redemptive purposes. To some degree, culture both forms us and is transformed by us. Christians dare not accept the secular attempts to push Christians out of the public square. Instead, we are to engage in

---

the tools, the conventions, the social ties, and all else contributing to this call. Cultural activity occurs in a historical setting, and is meant to improve the human condition" (Edgar, *Created and Creating*, 233).

5. Edgar, *Created and Creating*, 168.

6. Edgar, *Created and Creating*, 212.

the sciences, the arts, scholarship and education, economics, and politics and government in decidedly Christian ways.[7]

GOVERNMENT

Government is both downstream of culture and a great shaper of culture. Government isn't "a necessary evil" but one aspect of the dominion we humans exercise. Adam governed in the garden. But ever since the fall in sin, human civilizations have been governed by fallen, very fallible humans.

Following the flood, God instructed Noah in basics of how humans are to govern justly: "And for your lifeblood I will require a reckoning: from every beast I will require it and from man. From his fellow man I will require a reckoning for the life of man. Whoever sheds the blood of man, by man shall his blood be shed, for God made man in his own image" (Gen 9:5–6). For humanity to be able to function and flourish and fulfill the cultural mandate to be fruitful and multiply (Gen 9:7), humans need at least minimum government to uphold justice. Since humans are created in the image of God, God instituted the death penalty for those who attacked God's image bearers, since murder is a direct assault upon the God whose image we bear and because murder is a threat to civilization.

One of the examples of a very fallible human civilization and government after the flood is Nimrod. In Genesis 10:8–12, we read,

> Cush fathered Nimrod; he was the first on earth to be a mighty man. He was a mighty hunter before the LORD. Therefore it is said, "Like Nimrod a mighty hunter before the LORD." The beginning of his kingdom was Babel, Erech, Accad, and Calneh, in the land of Shinar. From that land he went into Assyria and built Nineveh, Rehoboth-Ir, Calah, and Resen between Nineveh and Calah; that is the great city.

7. For a simple, basic study regarding Christian cultural engagement, see Ashford, *Every Square Inch*.

Nimrod built cities. He was the founder of Babel in the land of Shinar. As Genesis 11:1–9 records, Babel was a great city in which people sought to make a name for themselves. It was a city governed not according to God's purposes but for their own godless ends.

In contrast to the cities of man, like Babel, God chose Abraham and his descendants, and he gave Israel his law (Torah) so that they might be a nation governed according to God's commandments. Israel reached its zenith under the reigns of King David and his son, King Solomon. First Kings 4 and 1 Chronicles 27, for instance, record the vast, organized government led by King David and King Solomon. While the point of these passages isn't to say that big government bureaucracy is better than small government, we see in such texts that humans need wise and proportionate government to maintain righteousness and justice so that humans may flourish.

The Bible recognizes that human governments can be murderous, even destructive to human flourishing (Dan 7:1–8). Yet God's ultimate purposes and plans come to fruition through the wise governance of "one like a son of man," Jesus Christ (Dan 7:13). With his saving work finished, this One comes before God, "and to him was given dominion and glory and a kingdom, that all peoples, nations, and languages should serve him; his dominion is an everlasting dominion, which shall not pass away, and his kingdom one that shall not be destroyed" (Dan 7:14). This Son of Man is David's greater Son. In Isaiah we're told "the government shall be upon his shoulder, and his name shall be called Wonderful Counselor, Mighty God, Everlasting Father, Prince of Peace. Of the increase of his government and of peace there will be no end, on the throne of David and over his kingdom, to establish it and to uphold it with justice and with righteousness from this time forth and forevermore" (Isa 9:6–7). He shall reign at the right hand of God until all his enemies are defeated (Ps 110:1). Jesus will govern forever as the King of kings and Lord of lords for the good of his people.

Until he returns, Jesus sovereignly reigns and accomplishes his purposes through faulty, frail, fallible human governments. As Jesus himself made clear, human governments have their rightful sphere of influence. It's right and good to pay taxes and to honor and respect those whom God places over us (Matt 22:15–22; see also 1 Pet 2:13–17). Yet there is a limit to the government's sphere of authority and influence. As good citizens, we're to render to Caesar what bears his image and therefore belongs to Caesar, but we bear God's image, so we are to render to God ourselves and our final allegiance (Matt 22:20–21). When a government's dictates conflict with God, we must obey God rather than men (Acts 5:29). But our natural response to those in authority over us should be submission and respect, thanking God for them and praying for them (Exod 20:12, Rom 13:1, 1 Tim 2:1–2).

God has given government as a good gift for the good of his people: "That we may lead a peaceful and quiet life, godly and dignified in every way" (1 Tim 2:2). Every rightful authority is from God and has been instituted by him (Rom 13:1). To resist rightful laws and legitimate governance is to rebel against God and incur the rightful wrath of God through his appointed agent (Rom 13:2–4). The government bears the sword—to protect its citizens from outside threats through war and from threats to justice from within. Though Jesus does not permit personal vengeance, the government's job is to fulfill God's mandate for proportionate justice by avenging its citizens who are wronged to maintain a functional society (Matt 5:38–46, Rom 13:4).

Through just governance, image-bearing humans serve image-bearing humans in this age. Government thus enables humans to fulfill our God-given callings and to form and transform culture for Christ's redemptive purposes.[8] Governments allow human beings to fulfill God's potential to show his infinite, manifold wisdom through our creativity and loving service toward one another and the creation we oversee as we await the return of Jesus.

Whether in vocation, culture, or in government, every human should do all to the glory of the God who created us, as we'll consider in chapter 12. And as Christians, we should do all to the glory of the God who also redeemed us (1 Cor 10:31). That doesn't

8. For a simple, helpful, biblical treatment of Christians and politics, see Ashford and Pappalardo, *One Nation Under God.*

mean that every song that's written has to be about Jesus nor that every painting needs to be specifically religious. We should worship God in all of life in everything that we do, doing it in a manner that reflects the beauty, goodness, and righteousness of God. There's a place for art and song, for example, to reflect the ugliness of sin and the injustices we see in the world. Yet it should still be done with modesty and hope. As God's creatures, made and redeemed to represent God, everything that we do should serve that very purpose: to reflect God for his glory.

11

"Don't Die"

The Human Quest to Live Forever and the Promise of God

"Don't Die." That's what the T-shirt reads on Bryan Johnson, the tech millionaire who believes that dying is optional. Johnson has spent millions of dollars and taken radical steps to reduce his "biological age"; he's "reframing what it means to be human."[1] Believing that AI will give humans the proper algorithms to biologically live forever, Johnson has entrusted himself to this technology (and seeks to make money helping others do so). For Bryan Johnson, humans are nothing more than chemically controlled organic machines.[2]

Bryan Johnson is an adherent of transhumanism. According to *Britannica*, transhumanism is the

1. Alter, "Live Forever," para. 4.

2. The article quotes Johnson as saying, "Whether we're talking about falling in love, or having sex, or going to the baseball game, you're talking about biochemical states in the body." Johnson says, "You can remove everything and just say, 'I'm experiencing this kind of electrical activity in my body and these kinds of hormones.' We have a whole bunch of ideas about what it means to exist, we have all these ideas about what is happiness, and other things" (Alter, "Live Forever," para. 24).

> philosophical and scientific movement that advocates the use of current and emerging technologies—such as genetic engineering, cryonics, artificial intelligence (AI), and nanotechnology—to augment human capabilities and improve the human condition. Transhumanists envision a future in which the responsible application of such technologies enables humans to slow, reverse, or eliminate the aging process, to achieve corresponding increases in human life spans, and to enhance human cognitive and sensory capacities. The movement proposes that humans with augmented capabilities will evolve into an enhanced species that transcends humanity—the "posthuman."[3]

While adherents of transhumanism would likely deny it, transhumanism is really a religious commitment based on philosophical naturalism (the belief that all that exists, or at least all that matters, is the natural universe—there is no supernatural, such as God or the spiritual realm, or supernatural things are not important). Although scientists reject Johnson's conclusions, and even consider his practices unsafe, many people share his techno-optimism.[4]

Someone has said (and it's often attributed to G. K. Chesterton), "When men do not believe in God, they do not believe in nothing, they then will believe in anything."[5] Transhumanism is one form of "anything" that people like Bryan Johnson believe. As Christians, we should not be surprised at what Johnson and others are seeking to do. Ecclesiastes 3:11 tells us that God "has put eternity into man's heart." This is as true today as it was when written. If secular humanists had hoped that modern and postmodern secular societies and people would accept "fate" and give up on the religious quest for heaven or the mythical quest for the fountain of youth, they were gravely mistaken (pun intended). Humans continue to long for eternal life in some form or another. Transhumanism is

3. Rafferty et al., "Transhumanism," para. 1.

4. Alter, "Live Forever," paras. 18–19.

5. For a discussion on the attribution, see The Society of G. K. Chesterton, "When Man Ceases."

nothing new; just the latest quest for immortality apart from God that goes at least as far back as the Tower of Babel (Gen 11:1–9).

Transhumanism, and other attempts to overcome death, expose the ultimate convictions and commitments of humans. Ideas have consequences, including one's views of humanity, as I've sought to demonstrate throughout this book. If humans are merely highly evolved chemical machines, then much money and great effort will be expended to make these machines last longer or overcome the inevitable. If humans are part of the cosmic whole, then finding one's way to oneness in nirvana through yoga and transcendental meditation is the obvious answer. But if humans are sinful creatures made by a holy God to commune with God and one another forever or to be sent into everlasting destruction in hell, then redemption by God through Jesus Christ is the only solution.

LONGING FOR MORE

The words of Ecclesiastes 3:11 explain why humans are dissatisfied with this short life: God has put eternity into our hearts. Biblical commentator Michael Eaton explains,

> The eternity of God's dealings with mankind corresponds to something inside us: we have a capacity for eternal things, are concerned about the future, want to understand "from the beginning to the end," and have a sense of something which transcends our immediate situation.[6]

We have a longing to live forever that goes beyond reason. That is why people continue to look for ways to escape death and live forever, even with the scientism and rationalism that has dominated Western civilizations since the so-called "Enlightenment."

Rather than trying to come up with materialistic, evolutionary explanations for why people want to live forever, we need to point them to the truth: humans weren't created to die. This desire

6. Eaton, *Ecclesiastes*, 95.

to live forever and to experience and understand eternal things creates a tension that points people to our need for the Savior.

As a pastor, I have done my fair share of funerals. I must admit, I do not like funerals. It's not that I don't enjoy the opportunity to minister to grieving persons or families nor that I don't treasure this unique opportunity to preach the gospel—as dying church members often tell me, their only desire at their funeral is for lost loved ones to hear the way of salvation. Rather, I don't like how we Westerners treat such occasions. As I write, I'm preparing a series on the book of Lamentations for our congregation. While I have heard a few sermons on Lamentations in my life, I have rarely heard a message on lamenting (though it's a regular topic throughout Scripture). I have never been taught how to lament, and as I'm reading to prepare, I realize I am not the exception. And this lack of understanding and embracing grief and lament as a good gift from God pervades funerals. Often, Christians say unhelpful (though well-intentioned) things to those who have lost loved ones like, "Don't cry. He/she is in heaven with Jesus and isn't suffering any longer." While that's true that a believer who has died is now with the Lord, mourning is not only natural but healthy in the face of such loss.

Death is both completely natural (in the sense that creatures, including humans, die) yet also completely unnatural. Death is not a part of life (but it's opposite). There is nothing more unnatural than for the image bearers of the living God to die. Death is the result of sin (Rom 6:23). And every death is a reminder of sin and that we live in a world still affected by sin.

Jesus came into the world to redeem his people—to save us from the inevitable consequences of our sin, as we saw in chapter 9. "Since therefore the children share in flesh and blood, he himself likewise partook of the same things, that through death he might destroy the one who has the power of death, that is, the devil, and deliver all those who through fear of death were subject to lifelong slavery" (Heb 2:14–15). Jesus died on the cross. He died to destroy the works of the devil so that he now has the keys of death and Hades (Rev 1:18). Death is no longer a locked door. Jesus has opened the door and is rescuing us, people who were trapped and enslaved to death.

As the perfect, obedient Son of God, Jesus rightly deserves eternal life. He now shares that eternal life with all of his brothers and sisters. But the eternal life Jesus gives isn't merely the quantity of life—living forever; Jesus gives abundant life, life as it's meant to be lived, in relationship with God (John 10:10, 17:3). Eternal life is a present reality for everyone who has a relationship with God through faith in Jesus Christ as Lord and Savior.[7] Those with eternal life are united with Jesus Christ, so even death cannot separate us from life with Christ (Rom 8:38–39). When Christians die, we are immediately, consciously in the presence of the Lord in heaven as we await his return and the final resurrection (see 2 Cor 5:6–9, Phil 1:21–23, Rev 6:9–11). When Jesus returns, he will raise his people to live with him in perfected, resurrection bodies in the new heaven and new earth (1 Cor 15:20–28, 35–54; 1 Thess 4:13–17; 2 Pet 3:11–13).

As Christians, we now live in light of this hope, detailed in Romans 8:18–25. There we read,

> For I consider that the sufferings of this present time are not worth comparing with the glory that is to be revealed to us. For the creation waits with eager longing for the revealing of the sons of God. For the creation was subjected to futility, not willingly, but because of him who subjected it, in hope that the creation itself will be set free from its bondage to corruption and obtain the freedom of the glory of the children of God. For we know that the whole creation has been groaning together in the pains of childbirth until now. And not only the creation, but we ourselves, who have the firstfruits of the Spirit, groan inwardly as we wait eagerly for adoption as sons, the redemption of our bodies. For in this hope we were saved.

7. In John 5:24, Jesus says, "Truly, truly, I say to you, whoever hears my word and believes him who sent me has eternal life. He does not come into judgment, but has passed from death to life." Notice, Jesus says that the one who believes *has* eternal life, already. When he says believers don't "come into judgment," he doesn't mean believers won't be judged but that Christians will not face God's wrath (see 2 Cor 5:10, 1 Thess 5:9, Rev 20:11–15).

> Now hope that is seen is not hope. For who hopes for what he sees? But if we hope for what we do not see, we wait for it with patience.

This passage is clear: we face sufferings during this "present time." We face loss, including the death of loved ones. Every moment we face the ticking clock ourselves—we face the breakdown in our bodies that even AI cannot stop, and eventually, death (see Eccl 12:1–7). So life is full of futility, frustration, and sorrow. We groan in these pains of life, yet we groan with hope, a hope infinitely greater than that of Bryan Johnson. In hope, we wait in patience. We can enjoy this life rather than making ourselves miserable trying to live forever in this world marred by sin and death. Even through intense suffering, we can worship God and rejoice in hope of eternal life (see 1 Pet 1:3–9). This is one reason why suicide and "euthanasia" are not viable options for humans, even when we face intense suffering.

HOPE AND DEATH

"Euthanasia," which transliterates the Greek meaning "good death," is becoming popular in Western societies. Sometimes "euthanasia" is termed "assisted death," or something like that, but it is always a form of suicide or homicide. As Christians, we must be clear that "euthanasia" isn't an option for us or for other human beings because, as we've seen, we are created beings under the providence of a sovereign God. God is in control, so he alone has the right, the authority, to determine how long we (and every human) lives. As the apostle Paul's words in Romans 8 imply, suffering is not sufficient reason to choose death, even for Christians who know that when we close our eyes in death we open them in the presence of the Lord.

"Euthanasia" is a lie of a secular culture that has embraced naturalism and sees human beings as valuable only insofar as they serve the "common good." Unfortunately, it's not long before the "right" to die becomes the "responsibility" to die, if people are viewed only in utilitarian terms. The only response to combat the dangerous, dehumanizing lies around us is with the truth of understanding human beings in the biblical terms we have considered.

Understanding humans in biblical terms also helps us to make end-of-life decisions. For instance, if a person is unconscious, being kept alive *only* by artificial means, and faithful doctors determine he/she will not return to consciousness, families can, with clear consciences and trust in the sovereign Lord, allow medical staff to remove the artificial means for keeping the person alive. A "do not resuscitate" order is also acceptable, if the person decides such in clear conscience. Christians likewise can use medicine or other technological advances to help enhance or sustain health and life; but we do so acknowledging their limits rather than treating them as demigods.

Furthermore, Christians ought to seek burial, as burial honors and dignifies the physical body and the person as we await the resurrection. Yet for those who cannot financially afford to bury (for example), cremation is not a sin. We have confidence that God can raise the dead whether the body is burned up or buried and decayed.

But perhaps we must return to the attempt to live forever by our own means and ask the hardest, most soul-searching question: "Why?" Why, for what purpose and end, do "transhumanists" want to live forever? Is it because they fear death? Perhaps we as Christians can honestly pose this question to people who we know who share such fears. As Davey Jones asked Captain Jack Sparrow in *Pirates of the Caribbean*, "Do you fear death?" To which Sparrow responded, "You have no idea."[8] We may find out that people fear death because it's unknown or, more likely, because God has put within them a fear of the coming judgment; and no matter how hard they try to silence their consciences, they just can't escape the reality because they are human persons, created in the image and likeness of God. This fear can give us an opportunity to give a reason for our own hope (1 Pet 3:15).

8. Verbinski, *At World's End*, 1:52:23–26.

But not only do we have to consider the reasons for wanting to not die, but we must consider the purpose, the end, for someone wanting to live forever. Is the goal self-serving? If so, living forever will never be enough. "Even though he should live a thousand years twice over, yet enjoy no good—do not all go to the one place?" (Eccl 6:6). Living for self will never satisfy because it goes against the very core of our purpose. Living forever for self, in a world full of unavoidable misery and pain, would not be eternal life but a futile, vain fate like that of the Greek mythological character Sisyphus, who forever strains to push a rock up a hill only to get to the top and have it roll back down.

How can we humans live a meaningful, joyful life, both in this age and forever? It is to this question that we turn in our final chapter.

12

The Purpose of Man

WHY DO WE EXIST? Why are we here? What is our purpose? Your view of what it means to be human will determine your answer to these questions. But the reverse is also true: how you answer this question will affect your understanding of what it means to be human.

The writer of Ecclesiastes defines our purpose as follows: "The end of the matter; all has been heard. Fear God and keep his commandments, for this is the whole duty of man. For God will bring every deed into judgment, with every secret thing, whether good or evil" (Eccl 12:13–14). Because God has created us, he alone can define who we are, why we exist, and how we're to live. And God alone can judge, and he will judge, whether each of us fulfills the purpose for which he created us.

Similarly, the Westminster Shorter Catechism asks, "What is the chief end of man?" Answer: "Man's chief end is to glorify God, and to enjoy him forever."[1] Because we are created in the image and likeness of God, we exist to joyfully glorify God in relationship with him. We are inescapably *homo adorans*: "worshiping man."[2]

1. Puritan Reformed Theological Seminary, "Westminster Shorter Catechism," Q&A 1.

2. Wikipedia, "Christian Worship," para. 1.

We will worship something or someone. And whatever we worship will determine what we live for.

Understanding the purpose of man is essential to living truly human lives. Though I have assumed it throughout the book, I end with the purpose of man to tie every chapter together and to prepare for a concluding exhortation.

JESUS' PURPOSE

As we saw in chapter 2, Jesus is the paradigm, the model of true humanity. In understanding our purpose, we must begin with Jesus. Did Jesus live for the glory of God?

As Jesus entered Jerusalem the Sunday before his crucifixion, his soul was troubled because he knew what was coming. Yet he would not shrink back from this "hour." Jesus said, "For this purpose I have come to this hour" (John 12:27). What is Jesus' purpose? To die on the cross to save sinners, right? Yes, but there's more. Jesus continues with a brief prayer: "Father, glorify your name" (John 12:28). Jesus' ultimate purpose wasn't man-centered but God-centered, and these two purposes don't conflict (saving sinners and God's glory). Rather, Jesus came into the world to save sinners to fulfill the ultimate purpose: to glorify God.

Later that week, as Jesus prepared to go to the cross, he honed his purpose with laser focus. He prayed, "Father, the hour has come; glorify your Son that the Son may glorify you" (John 17:1). Knowing that the time had come to fulfill his purpose for coming into the world, Jesus again didn't shrink back. He pressed on to the cross, asking his Father to glorify him for a purpose: so that he may glorify the Father. Jesus lived for the glory of God until his dying breath. He says, "I glorified you on earth, having accomplished the work that you gave me to do" (John 17:4).

Though obedience to God is the duty of man (Eccl 12:13), that doesn't mean it has to be a chore. Jesus delighted in his Father and likewise obeyed him, fulfilling his duty with great delight. As the Father's true and ultimate representative, Jesus could say, "I have manifested your name to the people whom you gave me out of the world" (John 17:6). He perfectly represented the Father as the God-Man (see John 14:8–11, Heb 1:2–3). Obeying God and representing him is the purpose of humanity in the image and likeness of God. Glorifying God and enjoying him is what God created us to do, so it should be no surprise to read that Jesus, the true Man, perfectly obeyed his Father and joyfully glorified him.

GOD GLORIFIES GOD

Understanding Jesus' purpose leads us to ask, "Why did God create humans to glorify God?" One answer is because God created all things and rules over all things. As Creator, God alone is worthy of all glory. As the "elders" around God's throne worship, they cry out, "Worthy are you, our Lord and God, to receive glory and honor and power, for you created all things, and by your will they existed and were created" (Rev 4:11). Likewise, after contemplating God's amazing saving plans and purposes, the apostle Paul can't help but respond in praise:

> Oh, the depth of the riches and wisdom and knowledge of God! How unsearchable are his judgments and how inscrutable his ways! "For who has known the mind of the Lord, or who has been his counselor?" "Or who has given a gift to him that he might be repaid?" For from him and through him and to him are all things. To him be glory forever. Amen. (Rom 11:33–36)

God created all things for his glory, and that is why we humans exist for his glory.

Not only does all creation exist for God's glory, but God himself always seeks his glory. While that may on the surface sound self-seeking and contemptible, consider for a moment the alternative. If worshiping and glorifying anything but the true God is idolatry and breaks the first and greatest commandment, then how could God possibly do anything besides seek his own glory?[3]

3. This is true both for the Ten Commandments and what Jesus calls "the first and great commandment." The first commandment of the ten is "You shall have no other gods before me" (Exod 20:3). Jesus says, "You shall love the Lord

Scripture clearly states that God acts for his own glory (or his own name's sake). In Isaiah 48:11, as God promises Israel that he will act to redeem them, God states, "For my own sake, for my own sake, I do it, for how should my name be profaned? My glory I will not give to another." Likewise, in promising to save his people by renewing them from within, God told the prophet Ezekiel to say,

> Thus says the Lord GOD: It is not for your sake, O house of Israel, that I am about to act, but for the sake of my holy name, which you have profaned among the nations to which you came. And I will vindicate the holiness of my great name, which has been profaned among the nations, and which you have profaned among them. And the nations will know that I am the LORD, declares the Lord GOD, when through you I vindicate my holiness before their eyes. (Ezek 36:22–23)

God does all things for his own glory because he alone is worthy. And if God does everything for his own glory, and we are created in the image and likeness of God, it only follows that we too exist for the purpose of glorifying God.

HOW TO GLORIFY GOD

So how do we glorify God? First, it's important to understand what it means to glorify God. The Hebrew word translated "glory" is *kabod*, meaning honor, splendor, heaviness, or gravity.[4] So to glorify God means to treat God with honor, as the one who has the most gravitas and dignity, the most weight in your life. To glorify God then means for God to have first place, your full and final allegiance.

John Piper gives a helpful definition. Piper says to glorify God "means feeling and thinking and acting in ways that reflect

---

your God with all your heart and with all your soul and with all your mind. This is the great and first commandment" (Matt 22:37–38). Obviously these are not in contradiction. Jesus sums up the main thrust of the commandments, using Moses' own words (see Deut 6:5, Lev 19:18, respectively).

4. Weinfeld, "kāḇôḏ," 23.

his greatness, that make much of God, that give evidence of the supreme greatness of all his attributes and the all-satisfying beauty of his manifold perfections."[5] So glorifying God relates to every aspect of our person: what we think, how we feel, what we say and do, and how we say and do it. As 1 Corinthians 10:31 says, "Whether you eat or drink, or whatever you do, do all to the glory of God." Since glorifying and enjoying God is the purpose for which we exist, it should be no surprise that all of life is about glorifying God.

This is why glorifying God and enjoying God cannot be separated. We intrinsically glorify (treat as weighty) what we enjoy and delight in (what we value most). The French scholar Blaise Pascal wisely stated, "All men seek happiness. This is without exception. Whatever means they employ, they all tend to this end. . . . This is the motive of every action of every man [i.e., human]."[6]

Glorifying God then has two main venues in our lives: how we relate to God and how we relate to others (or the rest of creation). You should praise God with your lips. The psalmist says, "Because your steadfast love is better than life, my lips will praise you" (Ps 63:3). But it's not enough to just speak and sing God's praises, as the prophet Isaiah said, and Jesus quoted: God was displeased with Israel's worship because they honored God with their lips, but their hearts were far from him (Isa 29:13, Mark 7:6). They "honored" God with their lips, but they didn't truly love and value and delight in God. It's not enough to glorify God only with our words, we must glorify God by obeying him from a redeemed heart. If we love God, we will obey what he commands us (see John 14:15, 21). This includes glorifying God through sexual purity (1 Cor 6:18–20). Every aspect of life should be lived for God's glory.

We can also glorify God through how we treat others. As Micah 6:8 says, "He has told you, O man, what is good; and what does the LORD require of you but to do justice, and to love kindness, and to walk humbly with your God?" We can never separate glorifying God from how we treat others, just as we can never separate truly loving others from loving God.

5. Piper, "Glorifying God . . . Period," para. 3.

6. Quoted from Christensen, *What About Evil?*, 172.

So how do we learn to glorify God? Again, Jesus, the perfect Man, is our pattern. Though he's the perfect Son of God who never sinned, like all humans, Jesus developed. He was a baby, a child, an adolescent, an adult. All along the way, Jesus matured in a natural way. According to Luke 2:52, "Jesus increased in wisdom and in stature and in favor with God and man."

Obedience has levels that require maturity to increase responsibility. No one should expect a three-year-old to be able to wisely lead a manufacturing company for the glory of God. Obedience increases with knowledge, wisdom, and maturity. That is one reason an overseer of a church should not be a recent convert (1 Tim 3:6). A new Christian does not have the spiritual maturity to lead a church in the same way that a three-year-old doesn't have the maturity to lead a company. And in both cases, entrusting such responsibilities to one who is not ready will result in more harm than good.

Not only did Jesus grow in maturity through stages of life, but he also grew in maturity and obedience through suffering. Hebrews 5:8 says, "Although he was a son, he learned obedience through what he suffered." Jesus learned ever-increasing obedience through the sufferings that he faced so that he finally obeyed even to the point of death on a cross (Phil 2:6–8). Since Jesus, the perfect Man, learned through stages of development and through suffering, can we expect any different for any person? Of course not. God uses all things in life for the ultimate good of his people, to conform us to the likeness of Jesus Christ for Jesus' glory as the "firstborn among many brothers" (Rom 8:29; see also Jas 1:2–4).

Growing to obey God and glorify him through developing wisdom and maturity is how all humans increase in potential to glorify God, just as athletes increase their potential through training. Likewise, through the sufferings of this life that God ordains for his people, the result is increased maturity and obedience in increasing responsibilities. As humans, we are stewards of God's resources for his glory, whatever those resources may be that he entrusts to us (see Ps 24:1–2, 1 Cor 4:1–2). We learn to glorify God through God's sanctifying process of maturation.

God created mankind to glorify him, and we glorify him in increasing measure as our abilities to glorify him are developed. This flies in the face of the constant calls of our society to live for yourself and to do whatever makes you happy (when that "whatever" is not God). The Bible instead says, "Delight yourself in the LORD, and he will give you the desires of your heart" (Ps 37:4). The psalmist isn't saying that God will give you other things that you desire but that God will give you what you most desire and delight in: God himself. The result is that God is glorified in you, and you experience the deepest satisfaction and delight because you are fulfilling your true purpose. This indeed is the end and duty of man. This is the true worship of God that we see in the beginning and end of Psalm 8: the worshiping tongue of a human person in God's image exclaiming, "O LORD, our Lord, how majestic is your name in all the earth."

Conclusion

I'M A DRUMMER. AND as the old joke goes, the drummer is the guy who hangs out with the musicians but is not truly a musician. And yet, in my less-than-thorough studies of music, I learned the importance of resolution, of creating a sense of conclusion. So to resolve, I return to Psalm 8.

What is man that the God of the universe should be mindful of us? Three thousand years ago, Israel's King David asked and answered that question in Psalm 8. His answer is just as relevant today as it was then. David never could have imagined this "strange new world" that we face today, as Carl Trueman calls it.[1] And yet, amid the technological advances and moral revolutions, David had in Scripture the tools to address the issues we face today. How much more do we have the tools we need to face the issues of our own day, living this side of the fullness of revelation in Jesus Christ. God has determined the times and places in which we live (Acts 17:26). God has given us all we need in the person of Jesus Christ. As the author of Hebrews writes,

> In these last days he has spoken to us by his Son, whom he appointed the heir of all things, through whom also he created the world. He is the radiance of the glory of God and the exact imprint of his nature, and he upholds the universe by the word of his power. After making purification for sins, he sat down at the right hand of the Majesty on high, having become as much superior

1. Trueman, *Strange New World.*

> to angels as the name he has inherited is more excellent than theirs. (Heb 1:2–4)

God is mindful of us because his plan is to glorify his Son, Jesus Christ, the God-Man. And being mindful of us, God has shown us who we are and his will for us.

I trust this brief study on anthropology (the study of man) has been helpful for you. Through this study, I have attempted to show a simple, biblical understanding of mankind, why it matters today, and how a right view of humanity addresses many of the issues facing us and our society today. While this is far from a thorough treatment of either the subject matter or the issues we face, I have attempted to provide sufficient basis for you, the reader, to think critically and to speak intelligently to what you will encounter today. I have not shrunk back from showing how the Bible speaks to all the issues of our day, even issues that are controversial to both conservatives and progressives. If there are any errors, I own them as my own misunderstandings or miscommunications of the teachings of Scripture, which is the inspired, inerrant, infallible word of God.

As we have seen, humans, male and female, are created as persons in the image and likeness of God to reign on earth. Though we have sinned against our Creator, God sent Jesus to save for himself a people and to restore his creation finally and fully.

As the Bible began with God creating mankind to dwell with us in a garden-sanctuary, the Bible ends with God dwelling with his people in a garden-city-sanctuary. With the world cleansed from sin and everything and everyone that would continue to defile, destroy, and distort, all the peoples of the world live together in unity and harmony under the Lordship of Jesus Christ, the One Mediator. Together, humanity perfectly reflects the likeness of Jesus, loving God and one another, worshiping God together and basking in his glorious, revelatory light. With sin and death eradicated, mankind and the cosmos will fulfill in limitless joy the full purpose for which God created us for God's glory (Rev 21–22). That is the end. That is the goal for which God created man in his image and likeness to have dominion.

Until then, the Holy Spirit of God remains on mission, and the bride, the church, remains on mission, to see people reconciled to God and become like Jesus. If you have not yet been reconciled to God through faith in Jesus Christ as your personal Lord and Savior, God and his people are calling you to receive his grace. "The Spirit and the Bride say, 'Come.' And let the one who hears say, 'Come.' And let the one who is thirsty come; let the one who desires take the water of life without price" (Rev 21:17). Confess and repent of your sin. Believe in Jesus Christ and be forgiven and reconciled to God.

If you have been reconciled to God through Jesus Christ, then God calls you to join him on mission and to fulfill the vocations he has entrusted to you within the cultural contexts he has providentially placed you. You are a steward, a manager, and nothing you do for Christ is in vain (1 Cor 15:58). The time is short, so live for the glory of God and not what is passing away. Jesus Christ is coming soon, and his reward is with him. Even so, come, Lord Jesus.

Bibliography

Alter, Charlotte. "The Man Who Thinks He Can Live Forever." *Time*, Sept. 20, 2023. https://time.com/6315607/bryan-johnsons-quest-for-immortality/.

Ashford, Bruce Riley. *Every Square Inch: An Introduction to Cultural Engagement for Christians*. Bellingham, WA: Lexham, 2015.

Ashford, Bruce Riley, and Chris Pappalardo. *One Nation Under God: A Christian Hope for American Politics*. Nashville: B&H, 2015.

Beale, G. K. *We Become What We Worship: A Biblical Theology of Idolatry*. Downers Grove, IL: InterVarsity, 2009.

Burk, Denny, et al. *Male and Female He Created Them: A Study on Gender, Sexuality, and Marriage*. Fearn, UK: Christian Focus, 2023.

Calvin, John. *Institutes of the Christian Religion*. Translated by Henry Beveridge. Grand Rapids: Christian Classics Ethereal Library, n.d. https://ccel.org/ccel/calvin/institutes/institutes.

Christensen, Scott. *What About Evil? A Defense of God's Sovereign Glory*. Phillipsburg, NJ: P&R, 2020.

The Council on Biblical Manhood and Womanhood. "The Nashville Statement." https://cbmw.org/the-nashville-statement/.

Crowe, Cameron, dir. *Jerry Maguire*. Culver City, CA: Sony Pictures, 1996. Amazon Prime Video.

Danylak, Barry. *Singleness in God's Redemptive Story*. Altona, MB: Friesen, 2022.

Duncan, J. Ligon, and Susan Hunt. *Women's Ministry in the Local Church*. Wheaton, IL: Crossway, 2006.

Dunlop, John. *Finding Grace in the Face of Dementia*. Wheaton, IL: Crossway, 2017.

Eaton, Michael A. *Ecclesiastes: An Introduction and Commentary*. Tyndale Old Testament Commentaries 18. Downers Grove, IL: InterVarsity, 1983.

Edgar, William. *Created and Creating: A Biblical Theology of* Culture. Downers Grove, IL: InterVarsity, 2016.

Fairbairn, Donald. "Breakouts: Theological Anthropology, Gnosticism and the Early Church." Presented at the 2025 EFCA Theology Conference. Video, 54:10. https://helps.efca.org/resources/breakouts-theological-anthropology-gnosticism-and-the-early-church-dr-donald-fairbairn.

Gentry, Peter J., and Stephen J. Wellum. *Kingdom Through Covenant: A Biblical-Theological Understanding of the Covenants*. Wheaton, IL: Crossway, 2018.

Grudem, Wayne. *Systematic Theology: An Introduction to Biblical Doctrine*. Grand Rapids: Zondervan, 1994.

Haidt, Jonathan. *The Anxious Generation: How the Great Rewiring of Childhood Is Causing an Epidemic of Mental Illness*. New York: Penguin, 2024.

Henry, Matthew. *Genesis to Deuteronomy*. Vol. 1 of *Matthew Henry's Commentary on the Whole Bible*. Grand Rapids: Christian Classics Ethereal Library, n.d. https://ccel.org/ccel/henry/mhc1/mhc1.

Hoekema, Anthony H. *Created in God's Image*. Grand Rapids: Eerdmans, 1994.

Kilner, John F. *Dignity and Destiny: Humanity in the Image of God*. Grand Rapids: Eerdmans, 2015.

Kostenberger, Andreas J., and David W. Jones. *God, Marriage, and Family: Rebuilding the Biblical Foundation*. 2nd ed. Wheaton, IL: Crossway, 2010.

Ligonier Ministries. *A Field Guide on Gender and Sexuality*. Sanford, FL: Ligonier Ministries, 2024.

Machen, J. Gresham. *The Christian View of Man*. Carlisle, PA: Banner of Truth Trust, 1984.

Mark, Joshua J. "Enuma Elish—The Babylonian Epic of Creation—Full Text." World History Encyclopedia, May 4, 2018. https://www.worldhistory.org/article/225/enuma-elish-the-babylonian-epic-of-creation-fu/.

Mathews, Kenneth A. *Genesis 1:1—11:26*. New American Commentary 1. Nashville: Broadman & Holman, 1996.

Merillat, Herbert Christian. "When the Two Become One." In *The Gnostic Apostle Thomas: "Twin" of Jesus*. 1997. http://www.gnosis.org/thomasbook/ch24.html.

Newheiser, Jim. *Marriage, Divorce, and Remarriage: Critical Questions and Answers*. Phillipsburg, NJ: P&R, 2017.

Piper, John. "Glorifying God . . . Period." Desiring God, July 15, 2013. https://www.desiringgod.org/messages/glorifying-god-period.

Puritan Reformed Theological Seminary. "The Westminster Shorter Catechism." https://prts.edu/wp-content/uploads/2016/12/Shorter_Catechism.pdf.

Rafferty, John P., et al. "Transhumanism." *Britannica*, last modified Nov. 28, 2025. https://www.britannica.com/topic/transhumanism.

Silicon Valley Reformed Baptist Church. "The Baptist Catechism." https://baptistcatechism.org/.

The Society of G. K. Chesterton. "When Man Ceases to Worship God." April 29, 2012. https://www.chesterton.org/ceases-to-worship/.

Troxel, A. Craig. *What Is Man?* Basics of the Faith Series. Phillipsburg, NJ: P&R, 2010.

Trueman, Carl R. *The Rise and Triumph of the Modern Self: Cultural Amnesia, Expressive Individualism, and the Road to Sexual Revolution*. Wheaton, IL: Crossway, 2020.

———. *Strange New World: How Thinkers and Activists Redefined Identity and Sparked the Sexual Revolution*. Wheaton, IL: Crossway, 2022.

Veith, Gene Edward, Jr. *God at Work: Your Christian Vocation in All of Life.* Wheaton, IL: Crossway, 2011.

Verbinski, Gore, dir. *Pirates of the Caribbean: At World's End.* Burbank, CA: Buena Vista Pictures, 2007.

Weinfeld, M. "kāḇôḏ" In *Theological Dictionary of the Old Testament*, edited by G. Johannes Botterweck et al., translated by Geoffrey W. Bromiley et al., 7:22–38. Grand Rapids: Eerdmans, 1995.

Wikipedia. "Christian Worship." Wikimedia Foundation, last modified Nov. 3, 2024. https://simple.wikipedia.org/wiki/Christian_worship.

———. "List of Gender Identities." Wikimedia Foundation, last modified Nov. 19, 2025. https://en.wikipedia.org/wiki/List_of_gender_identities.

———. "Sologamy." Wikimedia Foundation, last modified Dec. 5, 2025. https://en.wikipedia.org/wiki/Sologamy.

Wilkinson, Michael A. *Crowned with Glory and Honor: A Chalcedonian Anthropology.* Bellingham, WA: Lexham Academic, 2024.

———. "What Is Man? Looking to Christ for the Answer (Part 1)." Christ Over All, Jan. 20, 2025. https://christoverall.com/article/longform/what-is-man-looking-to-christ-for-the-answer-part-1/.

www.ingramcontent.com/pod-product-compliance
Lightning Source LLC
LaVergne TN
LVHW020651100826
845148LV00012B/2427